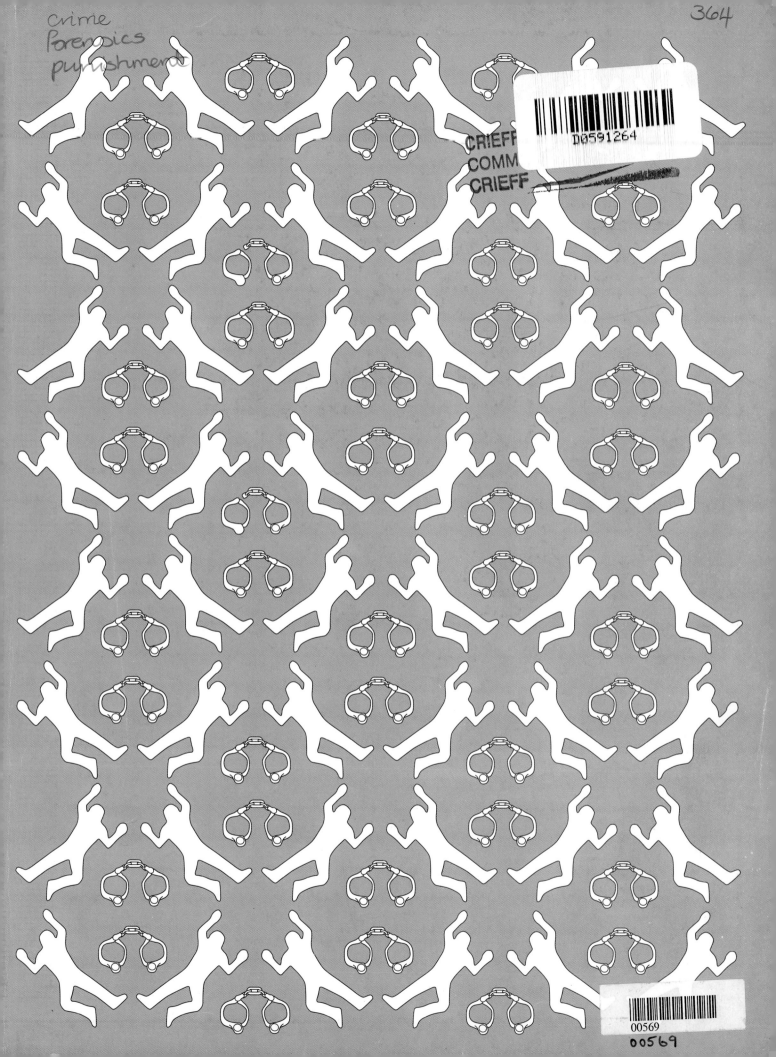

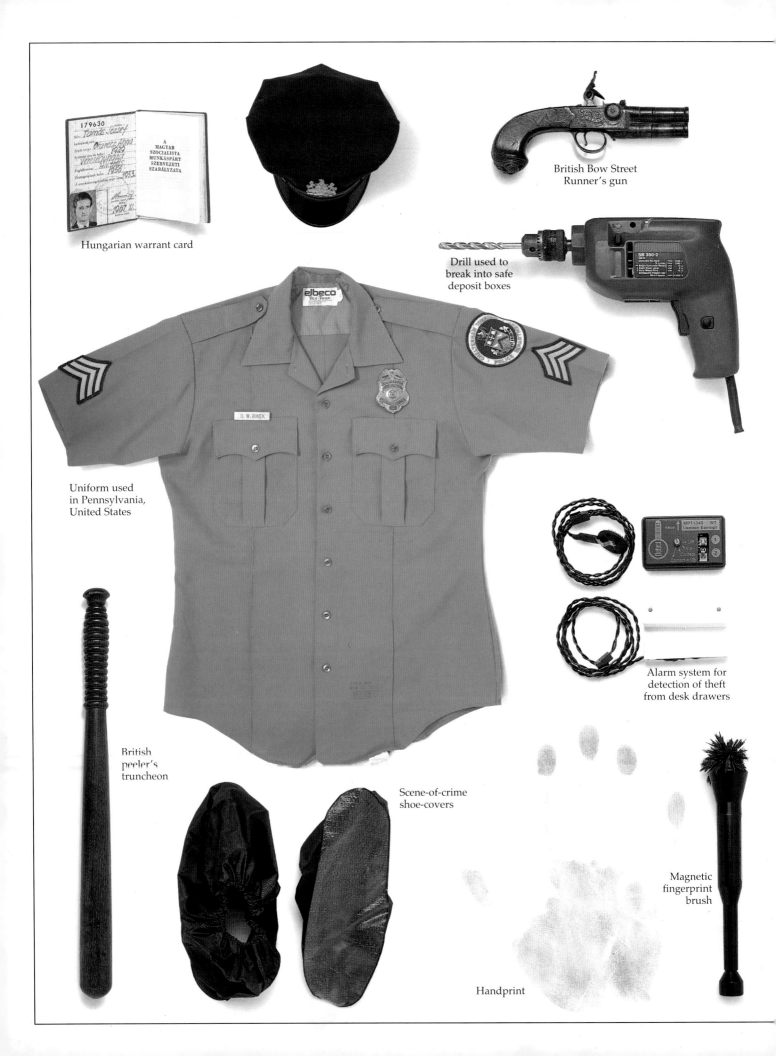

Hungarian warrant card

British Bow Street
Runner's gun

Drill used to
break into safe
deposit boxes

Uniform used
in Pennsylvania,
United States

Alarm system for
detection of theft
from desk drawers

British
peeler's
truncheon

Scene-of-crime
shoe-covers

Magnetic
fingerprint
brush

Handprint

US marshal's badge

British policeman's helmet badge

CRIME & DETECTION

Written by
BRIAN LANE

Photographed by
ANDY CRAWFORD

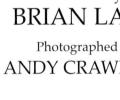

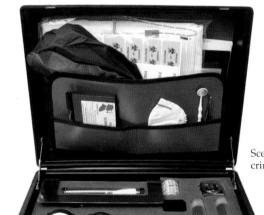

Al Capone's cigarette case

Black Jack Ketchum's handcuffs

Scene-of-crime kit

Dillinger's death mask

DORLING KINDERSLEY
London • New York
Stuttgart • Moscow • Sydney

British policeman's lamp (1930s)

Italian police cap

A DORLING KINDERSLEY BOOK

Project editor Kitty Blount
Art editor Carlton Hibbert
Senior managing editor Gillian Denton
Senior managing art editor Julia Harris
Production Lisa Moss
Picture research Sean Hunter
DTP designer Nicky Studdart

This Eyewitness ® Guide has been conceived by
Dorling Kindersley Limited and Editions Gallimard

First published in Great Britain in 1998
by Dorling Kindersley Limited,
9 Henrietta Street, London WC2E 8PS

A CIP catalogue record for this book is
available from the British Library.

ISBN 0 7513 6123 2

Colour reproduction by
Colourscan, Singapore
Printed in Singapore by Toppan

Policeman's rattle

Californian cloth
police badge

Policewoman's
truncheon

Truncheon

British peeler's top hat

Bonnie Parker's body armour

British peeler's uniform

Contents

Prison uniform of the type worn
at Alcatraz in the United States

Crime and society

THERE CAN BE FEW CORNERS of the world that are free from crime. Crime is defined in the dictionary as "an act punishable by law", so its nature depends on the laws of each society. The laws of a Christian society follow the teachings of the Bible; many of the moral values of Jewish and Christian societies are derived from the Ten Commandments. An Islamic society adopts the wisdom of the Koran. Among many African and Asian groups, tribal rules of conduct will often be decided by a council of elders, who decide both what is a crime and how to punish it. Despite the varying beliefs of different societies, there are certain codes of conduct common to them all.

CAIN AND ABEL
According to the Old Testament of the Bible, Cain, the elder son of Adam and Eve, was a farmer. He made a sacrifice of corn to God. His younger brother Abel, a shepherd, offered his best sheep. God accepted the sheep, but rejected the corn. From motives of jealousy and anger, Cain killed his brother. This, says the Bible, was the first murder.

THE AFTERMATH OF WAR
Wherever in the world there is war, there is destruction and lawlessness. In this confusion, some people steal goods from damaged houses and shops. They are called looters. The term comes from the Hindi word *lut*, which means booty. Looting also occurs during peacetime when there are inner-city riots. Closely associated with this crime is the secret selling of food and other items that are either generally not available or are heavily rationed. This is known as selling on the black market.

EMPEROR JUSTINIAN
Flavius Anicus Sabbaticus Justinianus, called Justinian the Great (483–565), was a Byzantine emperor who laid the foundations of Roman law. On these laws much of the modern world's legal systems are based.

The Artful Dodger picks a pocket while Oliver looks on in horror in a scene from Charles Dickens' novel Oliver Twist

DRACONIAN LAWS
Above is an extract in the original Greek of Draco's *Laws on Murder*. Draco was a lawmaker in Athens, Greece (624–621BCE). He made execution for all crimes, including laziness, obligatory. He believed minor crimes deserved death and he could not find a greater punishment for more serious crimes. The term Draconian laws evolved from Draco's harshness.

19TH-CENTURY CRIME WAVE
The increasing wealth of factory owners brought about by the Industrial Revolution in Europe widened the gap between rich and poor, and crime grew. This illustration from *Oliver Twist* by Charles Dickens shows some pickpockets in operation. It was partly this increase in crime that led to the founding of police forces and the strengthening of laws and punishments. In the first quarter of the 19th century, there were 156 crimes in England punishable by death, including heretical preaching and monopolizing corn.

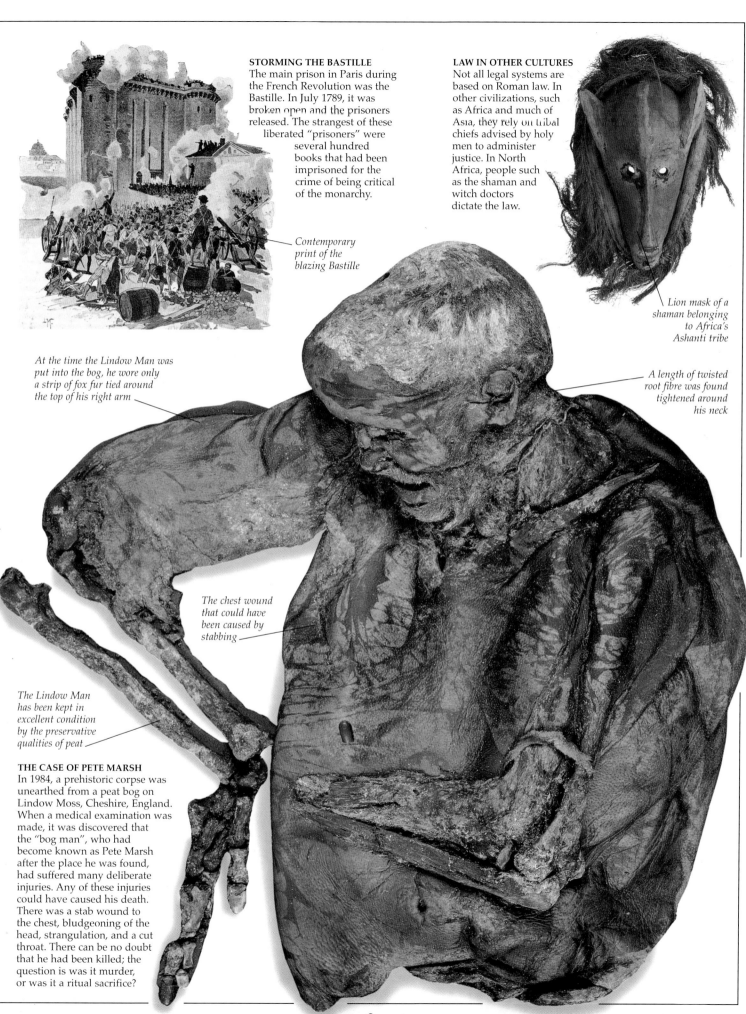

STORMING THE BASTILLE
The main prison in Paris during the French Revolution was the Bastille. In July 1789, it was broken open and the prisoners released. The strangest of these liberated "prisoners" were several hundred books that had been imprisoned for the crime of being critical of the monarchy.

Contemporary print of the blazing Bastille

LAW IN OTHER CULTURES
Not all legal systems are based on Roman law. In other civilizations, such as Africa and much of Asia, they rely on tribal chiefs advised by holy men to administer justice. In North Africa, people such as the shaman and witch doctors dictate the law.

Lion mask of a shaman belonging to Africa's Ashanti tribe

At the time the Lindow Man was put into the bog, he wore only a strip of fox fur tied around the top of his right arm

A length of twisted root fibre was found tightened around his neck

The chest wound that could have been caused by stabbing

The Lindow Man has been kept in excellent condition by the preservative qualities of peat

THE CASE OF PETE MARSH
In 1984, a prehistoric corpse was unearthed from a peat bog on Lindow Moss, Cheshire, England. When a medical examination was made, it was discovered that the "bog man", who had become known as Pete Marsh after the place he was found, had suffered many deliberate injuries. Any of these injuries could have caused his death. There was a stab wound to the chest, bludgeoning of the head, strangulation, and a cut throat. There can be no doubt that he had been killed; the question is was it murder, or was it a ritual sacrifice?

Law and order

IN THE SAME WAY that all societies suffer crimes, they have also developed systems of law by which to judge wrongdoers and assist the law enforcement officers to bring criminals to justice (pp. 12–13). Officers try to keep order in the first place by preventing people committing crimes and thereby breaking the law. In many countries, laws fall into two categories. One type is a law based on previous legal judgements. This is often an unwritten law and may be known as a common law. The other type of law is one included in a statute, which is a collection of written laws empowered by parliament.

Collar prevents garrotting, strangling from behind

Belt to which truncheon and lantern are attached

WOODEN RATTLE
A wooden rattle was used to signal an alarm or to call for help. Rattles were carried in a pocket of one of the swallow tails of the tunic. Rattles were originally used rather than whistles because hotel doormen used whistles to call cabs. By 1880, however, increasing traffic noise made whistles essential.

Lantern with thick, round glass front, like a bull's eye

Double-barrelled pistol of 1763 carried by a Bow Street Runner

Armband worn to show officer was on duty

Peeler's truncheon, sometimes called a nut-cracker

BOW STREET RUNNERS
In 1750, crime had become such a problem in London that Sir Henry Fielding, the magistrate at Bow Street Court, assembled a force of six men to patrol the street in and around the city. They were called Bow Street Runners because night and day they were available, within 15 minutes, to run after a criminal. Although they grew in number and effectiveness, the Runners were disbanded in 1829.

White, lightweight trousers worn in the summer

Peeler's hangar (sabre) and sheath worn on the belt only on ceremonial occasions

PEELER'S UNIFORM
Sir Robert Peel was the British Home Secretary from 1822–1830. He founded the Metropolitan Police at Scotland Yard. They became known as peelers or bobbies, shortenings of Sir Robert's name. The force was known for its distinguished uniform.

Stove-pipe hat, strong enough to protect the head and sturdy enough to stand on and see over a wall

THE FIRST FRENCH POLICE
Louvois (left) and La Reynie founded the police force in Paris, France, in 1667. La Reynie, chief of police, abolished the *cour des miracles*. A *cour des miracles* was an area of sanctuary in the centre of each French city in which beggars and bandits hid from the law. La Reynie also introduced a mounted and a pedestrian police force in Paris.

THIEF OR DETECTIVE
When the infamous French thief Vidocq was released from his last term in prison in 1809, he offered to act as a spy for the French police. He recruited other ex-convicts, who used their knowledge of criminal activity to make a very effective detective force.

THE STRONG ARM OF THE LAW
Tom Smith was a familiar figure in London's West End in the 1850s. He was 1 m 96 cm (6 feet 5 in) tall and weighed over 130 kg (252 lbs). It was said he could stop a fight merely by appearing at the scene.

Stove-pipe hat

Tunic collar with officer's identification number

This staff is tipped with a metal crown

SIGN OF OFFICE
Tipstaffs were used for identification. They were carried by English sheriffs' officers or bailiffs when delivering legal warrants. The officers themselves also became known as "tipstaffs".

Sheriff badge

Pinkerton detective badge

Federal Marshal badge

Plain jacket buttons

BADGES OF OFFICE
Public officials have always needed identification to prove their authority. It is especially important for law-enforcement officers, showing they have the power to search and arrest – whether a sheriff in the Wild West or a detective constable in London.

Pinkerton in disguise captures a thief aboard a train

ALLAN PINKERTON
Born in Scotland in 1819, Allan Pinkerton arrived in the United States in the early 1840s. In 1850, he founded Pinkerton's National Detective Agency in Chicago, which still exists today. Among other feats, Pinkerton foiled an assassination attempt on the life of Abraham Lincoln.

Frank James' revolver

Tassel from the furnishings at Jesse James' funeral

JESSE JAMES
Jesse James is among the most notorious outlaws in US history. Between 1866 and 1892, Jesse and his brother Frank headed a band of outlaws who robbed numerous banks, stagecoaches, and trains, and killed at least 10 people. In April 1882, Jesse was shot by Bob Ford, a fellow outlaw, for a share in the $10,000 reward for Jesse's capture, dead or alive.

Bullets dug out of a tree near Jesse James' hideout

A piece of Jesse James' coffin

Long trousers were worn all year round whatever the weather

Justice and sentencing

The prisoner, in blue, is being held by the arm

IN MOST PARTS of the modern world ideas of justice and sentencing go hand in hand. Justice is simply a means by which punishment can be given fairly according to the crime and the circumstances of the convicted criminal. The sentence is the punishment imposed. Most national laws take crimes of violence against people very seriously, and these offenses are naturally punished most severely. Violent crimes are tried in national, or high, courts. For lesser crimes, such as petty larceny (theft), justice is commonly administered by regional, or low, courts.

CHINESE COURT
A prisoner is brought before a magistrate in a 16th-century Chinese court. By that time, China already had a very efficient legal system based on the laws of Confucius, a famous Chinese philosopher of the 1st century BCE.

PILLORY
Putting minor criminals on display for the scorn and amusement of the public was first done by the ancient Greeks and Romans. In medieval times, a pillory was used. It trapped the neck and wrists of the felon. He or she was then displayed in the village square, or carried through the town. The public threw mud and rotten vegetables at the criminal; or, if they especially disliked them, stones.

LYNCHING
Lynching is the illegal hanging of an accused prisoner by a mob. The lynchers usually think that the prisoner will escape just punishment. Lynching can include beating, burning, or stoning before hanging.

Stroud's chess set and board, drawn inside the cover of his book Avian Anatomy

PASSING THE TIME
During his 54-year stay in prison for murder, Robert Stroud studied the diseases of canaries. He became a leading authority and wrote several books on the subject, including this one. He came to be known as "the Birdman of Alcatraz".

An English barrister, a lawyer who presents cases in court

"THE HANGING JUDGE"
The state of Arkansas had become so lawless that in 1875 President Ulysses Grant appointed Isaac Charles Parker as a federal judge in Fort Smith. During his legal career in Jesse James territory, Parker had developed a deep hatred for lawbreakers. In 21 years on the bench, Parker issued more than 160 death sentences, earning him the name "the Hanging Judge".

DEFENCE AND PROSECUTION
In many countries, an accused person is given the chance to have his defence presented to the court by a lawyer. A prosecuting counsel presents the opposite case, maintaining the accused's guilt. A jury, a group of independent, randomly selected people, decides whether or not the prosecution has proven the accused's guilt.

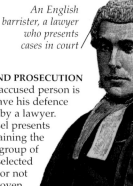

COURTROOM CAPERS
This scene depicts an English police court in the early 19th century. It is possible that the violent young men facing the magistrate were arrested for being drunk and disorderly. Such scenes are extremely rare in today's courts, partly because of the fear of harsher sentences, and partly because of the presence of trained security staff.

Handcuffs used to restrain Ketchum

"BLACK JACK" KETCHUM
Ketchum was born in New Mexico in 1866. He formed a gang that specialized in train robberies, but they had little success. "Black Jack" was a heavy drinker and not afraid to use his gun. He was finally arrested after being injured in a shoot out. He was convicted of the murder of Sheriff Edward Farr and hanged.

GUARD DUTY
This buckle is from the uniform of an Alcatraz guard. Either because of the fierce guards or the ferocious currents surrounding the island, only three inmates ever managed to escape the prison and they have never been seen or heard of since.

Alcatraz guard's belt buckle

Prisoner's number

Prisoner's shirt of the type worn in Alcatraz

"THE ROCK"
Alcatraz, the world's most notorious prison, was built on a rocky island in San Francisco Bay. Originally a military prison, "The Rock" served as a federal penitentiary from 1934 to 1963. Dangerous currents around the island made it impossible to escape. Famous inmates included Al Capone, "Machine Gun Kelly", and Robert Stroud, "the Birdman of Alcatraz".

Bounty hunters and thief takers

WHETHER BOUNTY HUNTERS in the US Wild West, or thief takers in 18th-century Britain, there have always been people ready to catch criminals as long as rich rewards are on offer. There were few sheriffs in the new, 19th-century towns of the United States, so bounty hunters flourished as rough-and-ready peace-keepers. Thief taking became popular in England after the passing of the Highwayman Act in 1692. This act offered large rewards for the capture of highwaymen and other criminals. If the thief takers were criminals themselves, they would be granted a free pardon for bringing in the accused. This meant that it was easy for a guilty person to send an innocent one to the gallows.

An idealized painting of Pat Garrett

A pouch of gold and silver coins, the thief taker's "blood money"

THE PAYOFF
Bounty hunters and thief takers were paid well. In Britain, a thief taker earned £40, and the highwayman's horse and goods, for each convicted thief. In the United States, the reward depended on the notoriety of the criminal – how well he or she was known for bad qualities or deeds. The first reward offered for Jesse James, the outlaw, was $500, the last was $25,000.

BOTH SIDES OF THE LAW
Jonathon Wild was one of London's most ruthless and powerful criminals. He also brought criminals to justice. Calling himself the "Thief Taker General of Great Britain and Ireland", he used a vast network of criminal informers to become the most famous thief taker London had ever known. He even sent some of his fellow criminals to the gallows. Wild was hanged in 1725, at the age of 43.

BILLY THE KID
Billy the Kid never went to school. Born in New York in 1859, he was brought up on the legend of Jesse James (p. 11). He became a gambler, rustler (a cattle and horse thief), and a killer. Billy's real name was William H Bonney.

TRACKER
In 1880, Patrick Floyd Garrett, the sheriff of Lincoln County, New Mexico, captured the notorious outlaw Billy the Kid. The Kid escaped from jail, but not from Garrett, who tracked him for three months, finally shooting him dead at Fort Sumner, New Mexico, in July 1881.

DICK TURPIN
As an infamous highwaymen in England, Dick Turpin was someone who made the Highwayman Act necessary. He tried to prevent his fellow-highwayman Tom King from being captured. In doing so, Turpin accidentally shot King, who later died.

Bullet-proof vest worn by many bounty hunters

An employee of a bail bondsman

Reeder Webb's ivory-handled Colt gun

Webb's leather-covered cosh

Sheriff Webb's knuckle duster

MODERN BOUNTY HUNTERS
In this photograph, a modern-day bounty hunter catches a criminal in Miami. More than 100 years have passed since the legendary days of the US Wild West. Although law and order is now firmly in the hands of the FBI and the local police forces, there is still room for the independent operator working for reward money.

SHERIFF REEDER WEBB
In 1927 the Texas Bankers' Association put out the announcement, "Reward $5,000 for dead bank robbers, not one cent for live ones". According to local legend, Reeder Webb, the sheriff of Odessa, West Texas, then lured two local thieves to a bank, where he shot them and collected the reward. To this day, a picture of Webb hangs in the sheriff's office in Odessa.

THE MAN WITH NO NAME
This still is from the western film *A Fistful of Dollars*. It is about an honourable bounty hunter. In real life, bounty hunters were mostly no more than hired killers, who would murder anyone for a fistful of dollars.

IN CUSTODY
Bounty hunting can still be a lucrative activity. In the United States, if a person is arrested and offered bail, he can borrow the money, called a bail bond, from a bail bondsman. If the accused does not appear in court, the bondsman loses his money. This is when the bondsman puts his bounty hunters on the fugitive's trail.

Theft and burglary

Suitcases can be used to carry stolen goods from the property

THEFT AND BURGLARY are known as crimes against property. The term theft covers everything from stealing an apple from a fruit stall to lifting a diamond gold watch from a jeweller's counter. The theft is far more serious if the victim suffers physical violence, as in the case of mugging. Burglary is entering a building for the purpose of stealing. It is considered a very serious crime, especially if the act was aggravated, for example, by the carrying of a gun.

MAKING A BREAK FOR IT
In 1950, a reformed burglar walked into the office of the English magazine *Picture Post* and offered to demonstrate his skills for the purpose of an article on how a housebreaker goes to work. He staged a job and it was photographed. The former burglar ended by saying that the general public made it easy for the criminal by not securing their homes properly.

COLONEL BLOOD
In England in 1671, Irish adventurer Thomas Blood and two others, disguised as clergymen, were allowed to see the crown jewels in the Tower of London. They attempted to steal them but found most of them too bulky and heavy. Blood managed to escape with the crown, crushed and hidden under his coat. The thieves were captured when Blood's horse fell. King Charles II, impressed by the daring of the plot, gave the robbers royal pardons.

NED KELLY
Born in Australia in 1855, the son of a transported convict, it was not long before Ned became a bushranger, a robber who lived in the bush, or outback. As the result of a scuffle with a policeman, he and his gang were hunted down by troopers. Only one of the soldiers survived the gun battle. For the next two years, Ned Kelly made a profitable living robbing banks. He is known for his remarkable suit of armour made by himself from iron. He met his death on the gallows in 1880.

Wanted notices

PUBLIC ENEMY NO. 1
In 1933, John Dillinger, aged 31, had already spent nine years in a US prison for theft. On his release, He formed a gang and became a notorious bank robber. Soon Dillinger was top of the FBI's Public Enemy list and huge rewards were being offered for his capture, dead or alive. Finally he was betrayed by Anna Sager, an acquaintance, who became known as "the woman in red". The FBI shot Dillinger dead as he walked out of a cinema in July 1934.

GREAT TRAIN ROBBERY

In the early hours of 8 August 1963, a gang of 12 robbers stole £2.5 million from the Royal Mail train travelling between London and Glasgow, Britain. They hid out at a remote farmhouse before separating with their shares of the loot. Three of the gang got away. The rest, including the three pictured here, spent lengthy terms in prison.

Train carriage

Charlie Wilson

Jimmy White

Bruce Reynolds

Headline announcing Dillinger's death

Dillinger's wooden "gun" blackened with shoe polish

DILLINGER'S ESCAPE

In the year preceding his death, Dillinger was arrested twice. Both times, he managed to escape. In Tucson, Arizona, he was convicted of possessing stolen money and firearms and sentenced to imprisonment at Crown Point. Always a clever crook, Dillinger escaped from the jail by waving a "gun". In fact it was simply a piece of wood carved into the shape of a gun. It could not have maimed anyone.

The forks can be levered up to here to allow the ram raiders to enter at a higher level

RAM RAIDING

A new threat hit the commercial and business world in the 1990s in the form of ram raiding. Vehicles fitted with fenders made from reinforced steel girders are rammed at the doors and windows of shops and warehouses, breaking open an entry for the robbers. The industrial vehicle shown above is perfect for the crime because of the forks at the front.

Dillinger's death mask. A mould of his face was made after death for identification

Drill could not pierce safe

SAFE DEPOSIT BOX OPENER

In 1987, £60 million was stolen from the Kensington Safe Depository Centre in London. This electric drill was taken to the scene to get into the safes. It snapped and was abandoned in favour of sledge hammers. Valerio Viccei, the leader of the robbers, was caught and imprisoned for 22 years.

Swindles and frauds

THE WORLD IS LIKE A LARGE MARKETPLACE, with people selling goods and services and other people buying them. But this atmosphere of commerce has another side to it. Wherever there is a chance to make "easy" money by dishonest means, there will be dishonest individuals ready to take that chance. And for every criminal, there are gullible people who believe that they can get something cheap. A swindle or a fraud involves deliberately cheating someone out of money. They range from card-tricksters at fairs fixing games so that it appears the client has a chance of winning, to con men who have managed to "sell" public monuments for huge amounts of money.

CHARLIE PEACE
A burglar and murderer of the 19th century, Charlie Peace moved in respectable and wealthy circles. He was able to live this double life because he was a brilliant master of disguise. Even his own family could not recognize him in disguise.

THE ULTIMATE BUG KILLER
Many swindlers do their business through newspaper advertisements. One, in the United States, promised "a method 100 % effective against cockroaches". People who sent their money received two blocks of wood with the instructions: "Place cockroach on block A. Take block B and strike down hard on block A". Although it worked, the fraudster was still sent to prison.

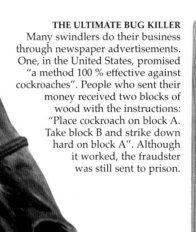

Block B, which is brought down on the execution block to kill the cockroach

FIXING SPORTS EVENTS
There are many ways to fix sports events, from paying boxers to take a fall, or football players to throw a game, to drugging horses to win or lose. The reason swindlers try to fix sports events is because of betting profits. They can make huge amounts of money by knowing in advance who is going to win, either by betting themselves, or by taking bets from others. Most sports are highly regulated to try to prevent this sort of manipulation taking place.

ALL AT SEA
False claims on insurance policies have always been a major cause of fraud. In earlier centuries this was a frequent crime in merchant shipping. For example, a ship carrying a cargo of wool is reported wrecked and the cargo lost. In fact, the ship would dock at another port where the wool was sold and the ship given a new name. The owner of the wool would have the money from its sale and the insurance money for its loss. The ship-owner would have both the ship and the insurance for its loss.

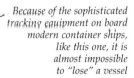

Because of the sophisticated tracking equipment on board modern container ships, like this one, it is almost impossible to "lose" a vessel

RESOLUTION BAY

PILOT

TWIN PROPELLERS

The queen of hearts is turned face down and shuffled among the other cards

FIND THE LADY

"Find the lady" is a confidence trick played in fairs or on the streets with three cards including the queen of hearts. The dealer lays the cards face down on a table, first revealing which one is the queen. He then shuffles them on the table, and invites the audience to "find the lady". A friend of the dealer's, pretending to be one of the crowd, puts money on a card, winning repeatedly. The public then try. But without having been briefed by the dealer, they cannot find the queen.

CHARLES PONZI

One of the world's most successful con men, Italian-born Ponzi, made a fortune in 1919–20. He persuaded people to invest money in his Financial Exchange Company with the promise of 50 per cent interest every 90 days. In fact, the company was not making any money. The interest it paid out was the money provided by the new investors.

George C. Parker sold the Statue of Liberty

Ponzi was convicted of fraud and served nine years in prison

Cockroach on its execution block

CREDIT CARD FRAUD

The most common credit card fraud is the use of stolen cards by thieves. Some schemes are more complex. For example, in the late 1960s, Alphonse Confessore, a maintenance engineer for Diners Club who was in the habit of making fraudulent charge cards for his friends, was blackmailed into printing 1,500 fraudulent Diners cards for an organized crime gang. Confessore was found guilty and murdered as he left court.

VICTORY BONDS

Horatio Bottomley from England was a swindler, publisher, self-styled "Friend of the Poor", and politician. He began the Victory Bond Club in 1919. This was supposed to let poor people buy a share in the government's post-war investment. In fact, he was not investing the money, just keeping it for himself. He made £150,000, was accused of fraud, convicted, and sentenced to seven years in prison.

SELLING MONUMENTS

Many of the world's largest and most famous monuments have been sold to the gullible by charming confidence tricksters. Probably the greatest "monumental" con man was US George C. Parker, who, over 45 years, sold the Brooklyn Bridge, Madison Square Garden, President Grant's tomb, and the Statue of Liberty.

Forgery

FORGER AT WORK
Decoration is added to a fake oriental vase. Chinese porcelain has always been a popular subject for forgers. Even modern artists' ceramic work is often copied.

THE WORD FORGERY is usually associated with banknotes. In fact not only money but anything that is rare or valuable is likely to be faked, from ancient Egyptian relics to modern "designer" perfumes. Forgery is not only attempted for profit, it can be for political reasons. In the time of the Pharaohs, some Egyptians forged the Shabaka Stone, which was intended to prove that the world was created in their capital city, Memphis. Some forgers, like those forging works of art, do so to deceive the experts. In former times, the forger was more likely to have success, but with the advance of scientific techniques and instruments, and the spread of knowledge, it is becoming more difficult for the forger to escape detection.

Gold-covered bronze

GUILTY GOLDEN EAGLES
This pair of fake eagle brooches were made in the 19th century, known as the great age of faking. The eagle design was popular in the culture of the Visigoths, a Germanic people of the 2nd–8th centuries. The originals were 12 cm (4.7 in) high, of solid gold with inlaid precious gems. Several eagle brooches were analyzed and found to be cast bronze covered with gold sheet and inlaid with coloured stones. In 1941, Amable Pozo, a jeweller from Madrid, Spain, was revealed as the faker.

A fake medieval medallion

Original shabti would have carried hoes; here they are mistaken for flail-sceptres

CASTING A FORTUNE
Shabtis were small figurines which were buried with the dead of ancient Egypt. Their purpose was to act as servants and carry out any tasks required of the deceased in the afterlife. Although some fakes have been cast from original shabtis, many have been remade. They are easy to detect because of clumsy detail and incorrect hieroglyphic inscriptions.

PLATED FORGERIES
These fake ancient "gold" coins, claimed to be from the time of Alexander the Great, were cast in copper and plated in gold. The fraud was only exposed when the plating split to reveal the bright green colour of oxidized copper.

Oxidized copper

Fake shabti

BILLY'S AND CHARLEY'S
In the mid-19th century, Billy Smith and Charley Eaton sold genuine antiquities dug from the banks of the River Thames, England. Demand was so great that they decided to make a few "antiquities" of their own, mostly "medieval" medallions. Despite being revealed as forgers, Billy and Charley continued in business until Charley died in 1870.

Shabti mould

THOMAS CHATTERTON
Chatterton, born in 1752, began writing his own poetry while still at school in England. In 1768, he wrote a fake medieval text. It was good enough to fool local experts. At the age of 18, he travelled to London and carried on writing fake medieval poems and letters. When some of his work was revealed as fake, Chatterton lost both fame and fortune. He took his own life with arsenic in 1770.

COMMERCIAL FORGERY

There was a time when perfume was just perfume. One brand cost about the same as the next. Now certain designer brands have become very famous and cost a great deal. Poor-quality copies of these products are made illegally. They are popular because they are cheap and have the appearance of quality.

When removed from the bottle it is bought in, one perfume looks just like another

COPYCAT CURRENCY

Forging currency can be very profitable. The forger can spend the counterfeit money or sell it to other criminals. The many precautions taken today, including paper quality, watermarks, numbering, elaborate engraving and printing processes, and security devices, make it more difficult to produce a forgery that can escape detection. But in earlier times, vast sums of forged currency circulated without detection.

A forged 1835 Bank of Rome note

A genuine 1835 Bank of Rome note

A fake Swedish 10-daler note, drawn by hand

FERNAND LEGROS

Legros is an eccentric French art dealer, recognizable by his signature wide-brimmed hat, beard, and dark glasses. In 1967, he was accused of having sold fake masterpieces to a now-deceased Texan multimillionaire. The canvases were painted by Hungarian forger Elmyr de Hory, who later committed suicide.

Hitler's handwriting

Hitler's genuine appointments diary for 1925

Julius Grant with one of the fake Hitler diaries

Comparison microscope

HITLER'S DIARIES

In 1983, the West German magazine *Stern* announced the discovery of the personal diaries of Adolf Hitler. Many experts lined up to authenticate them. Vast sums of money began to change hands for publication rights. Then Julius Grant, the greatest forensic document examiner of the century, inspected the documents. Grant soon determined that the paper on which the diaries were written contained optical dyes, which were not used in the manufacture of paper until after Hitler's death. Thus the diaries proved to be fakes.

Murder and kidnapping

PEOPLE HAVE BEEN HARMING and killing each other for property, power, or pleasure since the dawn of time. And other people have been trying to solve these wicked crimes. As people have learnt more about medicine and science, and laboratory equipment has been developed and improved, solving crime has become quicker and more reliable. This is especially true since the invention of DNA "fingerprinting" (pp. 44–45). It is now very difficult to commit murder without being caught, though it is often the criminal's own carelessness that leads to their conviction.

"ET TU, BRUTE?"
On 15 March 44 BCE, the Roman emperor Gaius Julius Caesar was stabbed to death in the Senate House by Marcus Brutus and his followers because they wanted to seize power. In one of the first triumphs of forensic medicine, Caesar's doctor Antistus was able to state that only one of the twenty-three stab wounds, the one through the emperor's heart, was fatal.

Le Petit Journal shows Detective Inspector Walter Dew arresting Crippen and his mistress, who is disguised as a boy

Le Petit Journal
ADMINISTRATION
5 CENT. SUPPLEMENT ILLUSTRÉ 5 CENT.
21ᵐᵉ Année — Numéro 1,030 — ABONNEMENTS
DIMANCHE 14 AOÛT 1910

ARRESTATION DU DOCTEUR CRIPPEN ET DE MISS LE NEVE
SUR LE PONT DU «MONTRO...

COMPLETE LIST
OF THE NUMBERS ON THE
CURRENCY
RECEIVED BY THE
LINDBERGH
KIDNAPERS

The Charleston National Bank
"The Old Reliable Bank"

LINDBERGH ABDUCTION
In March 1932, a baby was kidnapped in America. The baby's father Charles Lindbergh was the most famous aviator of his time. A ransom was paid, but on 12 May, the infant's dead body was found. He had been killed soon after the abduction.

Serial numbers from the banknotes were recorded before Lindbergh handed over the ransom money

Norman Schwarzkopf, one of the investigators, recorded details of the Lindbergh case in a diary

APPREHENSION OF DR CRIPPEN
Having poisoned his wife in 1910, Crippen left London with his mistress Ethel Le Neve on a ship for Canada. Despite the pair's disguises, the captain was suspicious and sent a telegram to Scotland Yard using the newly invented telegraph system. A detective overtook the fugitives on a faster ship and arrested them. Crippen was tried and hanged.

Dr Crippen's pocket watch

HAUPTMANN'S CAPTORS
In September 1934, FBI agents (above) learnt that some of Lindbergh's $70,000 ransom money had been used at a New York garage. The attendant had taken down the car number. This led to the arrest of a German-born carpenter named Bruno Hauptmann. Hauptmann was later tried, found guilty of the child's murder, and sent to the electric chair.

THE FRENCH "BLUEBEARD"
Henri-Desiré Landru used "lonely hearts" advertisements in French newspapers to lure wealthy women. He then took all their money and property, and disappeared. Those who refused were killed. Landru murdered at least 10 women between 1915 and 1919.

Landru and Madame Segret, his mistress, when he was arrested in 1921

Landru pictured at his trial at the Seine-et-Oise Assize Court in November 1921. He was convicted and sent to the guillotine

SADAMICHI HIRASAWA
On 26 January 1948, a Japanese man called Hirasawa murdered all 12 staff of a Tokyo bank. He posed as a Health Department official and told the manager that, because of a dysentery outbreak, all employees must be given a dose of medicine. Within seconds of drinking the cyanide liquid, the bank staff died. Hirasawa fled with 180,000 yen.

Hirasawa, imprisoned for murder

LEOPOLD AND LOEB
In 1924, Nathan Leopold and Richard Loeb, two American teenagers, tried to commit the perfect murder. On 22 May, they stabbed 14-year-old Bobby Franks to death and sent his father a ransom note demanding $10,000.
Leopold's spectacles were dropped near the body. This and other evidence lead to their conviction. They were sentenced to life for murder and 99 years for kidnap.

Lord Lucan's House of Lords cloak label

THE EARL OF LUCAN

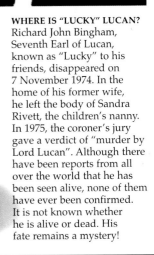

Lucan's trunk, in which he carried his silver to an auction shortly before he disappeared

THE Rᵗ HON
THE EARL OF LUCAN
No 5

WHERE IS "LUCKY" LUCAN?
Richard John Bingham, Seventh Earl of Lucan, known as "Lucky" to his friends, disappeared on 7 November 1974. In the home of his former wife, he left the body of Sandra Rivett, the children's nanny. In 1975, the coroner's jury gave a verdict of "murder by Lord Lucan". Although there have been reports from all over the world that he has been seen alive, none of them have ever been confirmed. It is not known whether he is alive or dead. His fate remains a mystery!

Prohibition

ON 28 OCTOBER 1919, in the United States, Congress passed the Volstead Act, which made the sale of alcoholic liquor illegal. At first it was a popular act, but soon it was found that Prohibition, as it came to be known, was both absurd and unworkable. People who rarely drank became desperate to do so; people who drank a lot demanded more. This demand was being met by organized gangs who had discovered that huge amounts of money could be made. Ships carried cases of spirits to the United States from all over the world. A $15 case of whisky would sell for $80. Rivalry between gangs was fierce and often erupted into violence in the streets.

AL "SCARFACE" CAPONE
Alphonse Capone, most notorious of the Chicago gangsters, began his career in crime in New York. In 1919, he took control of the illegal alcohol distribution in Chicago. It is claimed that Capone, with 300 gunmen, was responsible for 1,000 killings.

Al Capone's silver cigarette case

Crowd looting a store of confiscated liquor

HIDING THE LIQUOR
Soon the gangs found they could make more cash from distilling their own alcohol than they could buying it and there was less risk involved. However, many people tired of the excessive profits made by the gangsters and decided they too could make their own, known as "bathtub gin". It was not until 1933 that Prohibition was repealed.

A sawn-off double-barrelled shotgun hidden in a violin case

THE UNTOUCHABLES
Eliot Ness, born in 1902, became well known during the late 1920s as a special agent in the Prohibition Bureau of the US Department of Justice. He led a team of officers, called "the Untouchables" because they could not be bribed or intimidated by gangsters, to break up the trade in illegal alcohol.

HOOVER
John Edgar Hoover rose through the ranks of the US Justice Department to become the first director of the Federal Bureau of Investigation (FBI) in 1924. During the 1930s, he attacked the problem of gangsterism and started the "Public Enemy" list. Hoover ran the FBI for 48 years, under eight US Presidents.

SAM GIANCANA

When Al Capone died, other mobsters took over the Chicago underworld, such as Sam Giancana. Giancana later became the city's "crime boss". He moved into gambling clubs and ended up with a large share of the Riviera Casino.

Giancana after his arrest in Chicago, 1957, in connection with the murder of banker Leon Marcus

Giancana's lucky four-leafed clover

Giancana's lighter

GIANCANA'S JEWELLERY

Giancana's jewellery was confiscated and returned by the law many times. Before the age of 20, he had been arrested three times for murder. When he took command of the Chicago Mafia, he had been arrested 60 times for charges including battery, bombing, and assault to kill. He was described as the most ruthless mobster in the United States. In the end, he was murdered in his own home in 1975.

Giancana's betting book, containing winning slips only, was used as evidence of a legitimate income

CONCEALED THREATS

For obvious reasons, gangsters preferred to conceal their weapons when travelling to a "job". The most popular hiding place for shotguns and the Thompson sub-machine gun, or "tommy-gun", was a violin case. It proved surprisingly successful despite the fact a group of "Big Al's" hoodlums were not likely to pass as the string section of the Chicago Philharmonic!

Details of the various bets Giancana made

Frank Costello, born Francesco Castiglia in Lauropolin, Italy, became known as the "prime minister" of the mob

FRANK COSTELLO

Frank Costello rose through the US gangster world to control much of the country's gambling. In 1951, he was a star witness at the Kefauver Hearings. Despite the extent of his gangland crime, Costello, like Capone, was finally jailed.

KEFAUVER HEARINGS

The hearings were opened in May 1950 by Tennessee's Senator Kefauver. It was the hearings' task to see whether or not there was any evidence that an organized crime syndicate was operating in the United States. The five-man committee spent almost two years travelling the United States interviewing hundreds of underworld figures. Their conclusion was that such a network did exist.

International gangsters

IT WOULD BE WRONG to think that the Mafia is the only organized crime gang in the world. Wherever there is dishonest money to be made out of drugs, vice, gambling, and money-lending, gangsters will organize themselves into powerful groups to lay claim to it. Like the mobsters of Prohibition times, territory is jealously, and often violently, defended, and new territories are being established the whole time. For example, the Triads, who originated in China, now have units all around the world. However, there have been great changes in the way that these modern criminals operate. Gangsters often look more like bank managers than hoodlums, and many have come to realize that there is a considerable advantage in running a respectable business to act as a cover for their dishonest deals.

MAFIA NUN
Sister Alvina Murelli, aged 51, was arrested in 1983, when police in Naples, Italy, began their crackdown on the underworld of organized crime gangs. In her hand, she holds a copy of the New Testament's four Gospels. She used this to smuggle out coded messages from the mafiosi that she visited in jail.

MONEY-LAUNDERING
The main source of wealth for most gangs is the illegal trade in drugs. Drug barons usually turn their proceeds from "dirty" into "clean " money by filtering the cash through large "respectable" companies and banks owned or run by the gangs.

Paddle for turning cards

GAMBLING
Like drugs, illegal gambling is a popular source of gangland money. It provides very big returns for very little outlay, and the chances of winning are stacked against the player even if the game has not been fixed. Because the Chinese are fanatical gamblers, this money-spinner figures very strongly in the Triad economy, and basement gambling dens can be found in Chinatown districts around the world.

Card dispenser so that dealer's hands barely touch cards

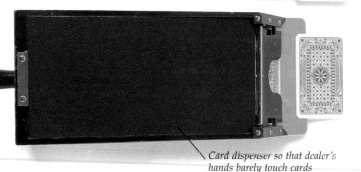

Betting counters known as "chips"

Gambling cards

YAKUZA FUNERAL
The Yakuza represent most of the gangland activity in Japan. Although they claim to have a Robin Hood image – robbing the rich to give to the poor – the Yakuza was officially outlawed in 1992 for its activities in the areas of extortion, money-laundering, and gun-running. In 1984, Masahisa Takenaka, leader of the Yamaguchi-gumi (largest of the Yakuza gangs) was killed by rivals. His funeral (left) was attended by members of the group – and 400 riot police.

Masahisa Takenaka

Giovanni Brusca was arrested at a seaside resort in Sicily

Doorway and steps carved out of stone

CAPTURING GANGSTERS

Improved communications systems around the globe have increased the efficiency and clean-up rate of most of the world's police forces. In 1996, the arrest of Sicilian bomber Giovanni Brusca ended one of the country's most intensive manhunts, and marked a significant victory against the growing threat of organized crime in Sicily and Italy.

Roulette wheels are often rigged so the operator can control where the ball drops

SECRET HIDEAWAYS

Communications between the Mafia bosses has also improved over the years, and many meetings are held to arrange "business" deals. In 1985, Italian police broke into caves under the country villa of Michele Greco, the top Mafia leader in Sicily. This underground hideaway was where Mafia leaders held summit meetings.

"RUSSIAN MAFIA"

In the confusion and disarray following the break-up of the former Soviet Union, organized crime moved in. Known as the "Russian mafia", the gangs have become ruthless and violent, and increasingly bold. This was matched with equal brutality by the police – resulting in many funerals such as that of "Mafia" man Vladislav Listiev (above).

ALL ON THE SPIN OF A WHEEL

One of the most popular gambling games, especially in the big casinos, is roulette. For decades, organized crime has found easy pickings at the roulette wheel, where corrupt casino owners run rigged games. Most of the profitable betting games, however, are played with cards – blackjack, poker, and faro among them.

Gamblers bet on where the ball will stop

Gambling chip

Chip sweep to gather in chips

Smuggling and piracy

SMUGGLING IS THE ILLEGAL movement of goods in and out of countries. It is a profitable crime because the smuggler avoids paying customs duties on these items. Customs duties are a tax on certain luxury goods, such as tobacco or alcohol, that are imported into the country. There is also a profit to be made when smuggling items or substances that are totally banned. For example, drug smugglers move illegal drugs, such as cocaine and marijuana, from one country to another. Another crime that crosses borders is piracy, or robbery at sea. Pirates have attacked ships since ancient times.

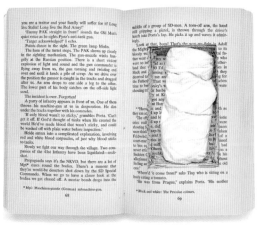

OLDEST TRICK IN THE BOOK
An old method of smuggling small amounts of illegal goods is to hide them inside a hollowed-out section of a book. Another method is replacing a legal substance, such as talcum powder, with a similar-looking illegal drug, such as cocaine.

Mandolin made from illegally exported turtle shell

ON THE EDGE OF EXTINCTION
As a result of the continuing threat to endangered wildlife, international agreements have been signed making the killing of certain birds and animals illegal. Also banned are the exports of some live creatures, and the trade in animal parts, such as skins, ivory, and bones. For example, the exquisite shell of a hawksbill turtle (left) is sold either complete, as a curiosity, or for making into souvenirs such as jewellery boxes.

Shell of hawksbill turtle

CUSTOMS OFFICERS
Policemen who operate at ports to prevent smuggling, such as these French officers in 1905 (above), are called customs officers. Early prohibited articles included alcohol and tobacco. While these are still smuggled, drugs are now often smuggled also.

FACE THE WALL
It was the custom among villagers of the English south coast during the 18th century to turn their faces to the wall when smugglers carried their contraband up from their boats. This way, the locals could not identify the smugglers when questioned by customs officers because such identification would both anger the smugglers and deprive the locals of the smuggled goods.

SKIN OF THE JAGUAR
This is the coat of a jaguar that was killed illegally. The skin was seized by the authorities in Brazil. In many parts of the world, the trade in illegal animal products provides an income that is vital for human survival. Where conservation is most needed, poverty is often at its greatest.

BAG CHECKING
While security officers look after the safety of a seaport or airport, the customs officers inspect the baggage of passengers for smuggled goods. Not every suitcase or bag is checked because officers operate on instinct, as well as information received, and can pick out bags likely to contain smuggled goods.

X-RAY VISION
In an attempt to reduce international terrorism and smuggling, equipment has been designed which will scan human beings and their luggage for objects, such as guns. This surveillance device has detected bags of cocaine, knife blades, coins, guns, and a plastic knife.

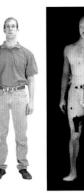

ALWAYS ON ALERT
Smuggling is not the only problem that air transport police must try to prevent. There is also the threat of terrorism and large-scale theft from the airport's secure warehouses. Airports are policed by armed security officers.

Space in a pair of boots to hide drugs

HIDING THE GOODS
Getting contraband (smuggled goods) past the watchful eyes of customs officers is the smuggler's most difficult task. There are very few ways that have not been tried – from the hollow book to the hollow spare tyre in a car. Others include shoes, statues, and ornaments as shown here.

A hollowed-out sculpture

Hollow heel in a shoe

Drum ready to be filled with drugs

PIRATES
The widespread piracy of the 16th to 18th centuries no longer exists, but attacks still happen occasionally in areas such as the South China Sea (above). Modern pirates usually attack merchant vessels and luxury yachts.

Fire! Fire!

Most fires start accidentally – a cigarette is left burning, or a cooker is left on. There are also fires that are started deliberately and these are called arson attacks. Whatever the cause of the fire, the procedure to put it out is the same. Most countries have an emergency fire service with fire brigades. When the fire brigade arrives at the scene of a fire, firefighters must make sure that any occupants are taken to safety, they must put out the fire, and ensure that the building is safe from collapse. If there has been any loss of life, or if the fire seems to have been started deliberately, a fire investigation unit is brought in to determine the cause of the fire. If arson is suspected because, for example, traces of petrol have been found, the fire investigation unit will work closely with the regular police force to solve the crime.

FIGHTING THE FIRE
Firefighters belong to one of the most dangerous of the emergency services. At each major incident there is a risk of three major hazards – fire and explosion, smoke inhalation, and falling debris. The firefighters' skill is enhanced by the use of well-equipped vehicles, and advances in protective clothing.

Glass storage jars are used for fire-debris samples because, unlike plastics, glass does not contain chemicals that could contaminate the samples

SAMPLE COLLECTION
Collecting clues is vital to the success of any investigation. Contaminated samples are useless for analysis in the forensic laboratory (pp. 46–47). Officers carry glass jars in which to store and protect evidence.

TESTING THE AIR FOR GASES
Once the fire is out, the fire investigation unit tries to find the cause. The hydrogen flame tester is used to detect the presence of flammable gases at the scene of a fire. Once it is established that a flammable gas is present, the gas can be identified and the cause of the fire determined. Within the machine, there is a naked hydrogen flame. Gas is sucked in and passes over this flame. The flame increases if the gas is flammable, and this increase is translated into a meter reading.
The degree of flammability indicates the nature of the gas.

Knob to adjust hydrogen gas flow

Reading shows how flammable the gas is

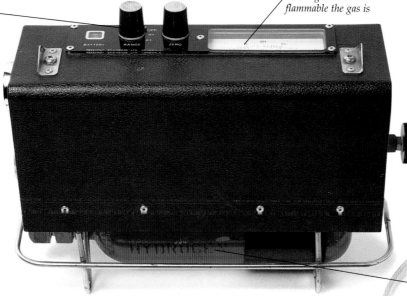

Hydrogen gas supply

Gas is sucked into the machine through this nozzle

Gas enters small holes along this tube

This extension tube is attached to the nozzle when detecting gases in awkward places, such as along ceilings or floors

REASONS FOR ARSON

There are three main reasons for arson. The fire may disguise some other crime, such as murder. It may be started as an act of revenge. However, the greatest number of arson attacks are associated with fraud. During the Great Depression in the United States in the 1930s, numbers of arson cases rose. A company having money problems would have its property burnt and collect the insurance.

Some people, like this man selling apples, did not resort to arson to raise money during the Depression

HEDGEHOG DISASTER

In Germany in 1954, Dr Müller and his wife were driving home. According to Müller, he left the car to remove a hedgehog from the road when the car burst into flames, killing his wife. However, petrol-can remains in the car, and proof of a love affair that Müller had been having, suggested this was arson. Müller was found guilty of murder and sentenced to six years in prison.

IDENTIFYING THE GASES

Officers use Dräger tubes to identify gases in the air. A tube of chemicals is inserted in the pump. Air is sucked through the tube by pressing the pump. If a gas is present, the chemicals will discolour. The gas is identified by referring to a colour chart.

Colour change suggests petrol fumes are in the air

Pre-test tube to determine presence of a hydrocarbon – it does not identify it

Sonic measurer

Tube to identify hydrocarbons, such as paraffin or petrol fumes

Metal detector

Indicates concealed, potentially dangerous, electrical wires, to be avoided when searching for clues

TAKING MEASUREMENTS

The accurate recording of a crime scene is essential to all investigations. This is especially important in the case of arson, where buildings may have to be quickly demolished for safety reasons. Measurements indicate the size and dimension of a location and the distance between objects. By comparing these measurements to the extent of fire damage, the officers can determine the speed and nature of the fires. A number of specialized measuring tools have been developed to give very accurate results. The sonic measurer sends sonic rays from one surface to another, measuring the distance in between.

External callipers

Vernier callipers

Magnifying glass with light

FINDING THE SOURCE OF THE FIRE

If the fire investigation unit have reason to believe the fire was started deliberately, a scene-of-crime officer, who specializes in cases of arson, will be brought in. As fires spread upwards, the officer will begin at the lowest point to find the source of the fire. Above, the officers are looking for clues by a window where an arsonist may have entered or left the building.

Meter gives a reading indicating the quantity of flammable gas in the air

Long rubber tube (through which the air passes) can reach into inaccessible places

PORTABLE GAS ALARM

The portable gas alarm detects gases in the air before they are present in large enough quantities to be a fire risk. It is used both in work environments that may be prone to leaking toxic gases, and by fire investigation units to ensure the atmosphere they are working in is safe. The hydrogen flame tester, left, is not used until it has been established that there is not enough gas in the air to cause an explosion when the naked flame is lit.

As well as the operating positions, the user can switch to "Battery" or "Alarms" to check that the machine is working properly

Squeezing this will send the air through the alarm system

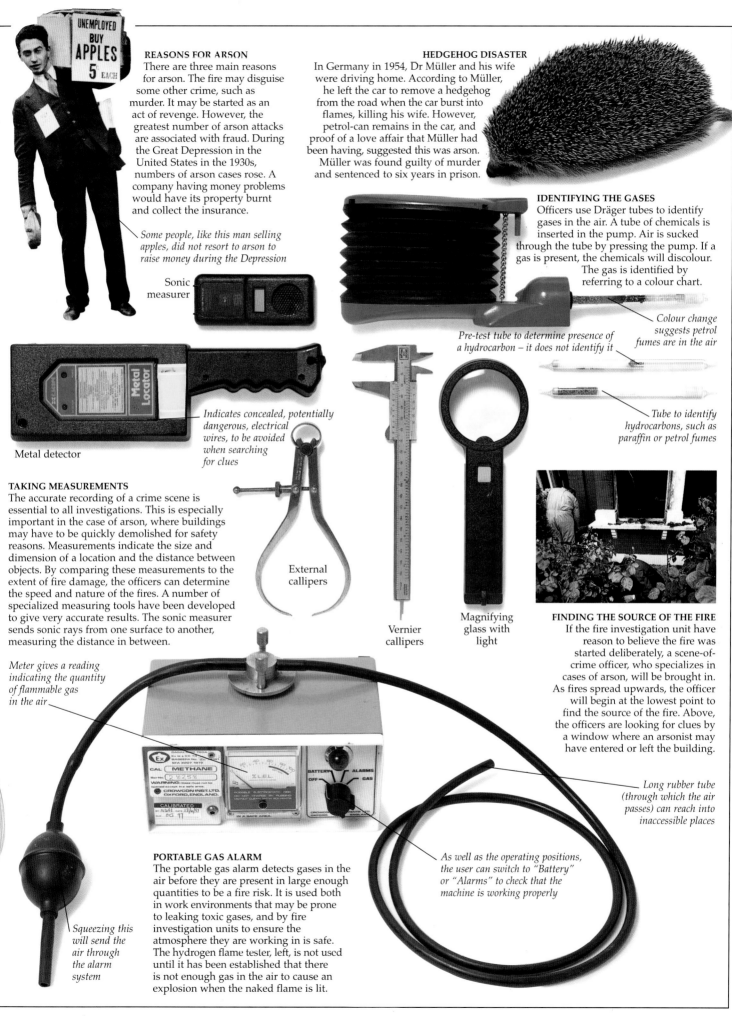

Police uniforms

THERE ARE TWO IMPORTANT REASONS why the police, and other emergency services, wear uniforms. First, so that they can be recognized by members of the public who need assistance, and by suspects being pursued. Secondly, so that they can identify each other and be identified by other services, such as firefighters, at the scene of an incident. As climates differ throughout the world, so forces have different uniforms to allow for it. However, while still being formal, uniforms are all designed to be comfortable and easy to move in.

Gendarme

US police cap with sun visor for hotter climate

A sergeant has a cloth badge of three stripes on the shoulder

HANDCUFFS
The "twitchers" were used to lead the condemned from court to cell. The clever French "come-along" was an earlier form of the modern handcuff. Leg-irons are a variation on handcuffs. These come from a cell in an early 20th-century prison.

"Twitchers" (1610)

Leg-irons (1902)

"Come-alongs" (1900s)

Police handcuffs (1990s)

US POLICE
This police shirt and cap were first issued to US sergeants in the 1990s. As well as the stripes of seniority, the shirt also carries a cloth badge showing the officer's department and the officer's own metal name tag.

A British peeler's rattle (1830s)

Truncheon issued in 1914 in Manchester, England

One star on the lapel indicates a constable

The German Niedersachsen state police force badge

WHISTLE ALONG
Although many modern police forces rely on car and personal radios for communication, whistles are still issued, usually for traffic control. These were issued in England in the 1990s.

Thunderer whistle

Acme whistle

New York night stick (1990s)

British woman's baton (1990s)

British side-handled baton (1990s)

England

Australia

Ireland

United States

Australia

New Zealand

France

United States

United States

TRUNCHEONS
Truncheons are used to help apprehend criminals. Their size and weight varies depending on the situation in which they are designed to be used.

OFFICIAL BADGES
Policemen all over the world have their own badges, showing which police force they represent. These cloth badges, attached to uniforms, were in use in the 1980s and 1990s.

GERMAN POLICE
This is the uniform of the Niedersachsen police force, one of Germany's eight state police forces. The badge on the left arm indicates which force is represented. One star on the lapel indicates that the officer is a constable.

Wide-brimmed Mountie's hat

Rope, called lanyard, that holds gun

Sam Browne (leather belt) and pouch

Gun holster

MOUNTIES
This familiar red tunic of the Royal Canadian Mounted Police was used in 1972. Originally Mounties not only upheld the law, but also acted as local counsellors and mediators. Their image has gradually changed and developed. In 1974, for example, women joined the Mounties.

Cap of the Russian militia

Silver badge of the militia

RUSSIAN
This cap and tunic belonged to a major in the Russian militia in 1989. The militia was responsible for policing Russia both before and after the break-up of the former Soviet Union in 1991. After 1991, Russia had to combat a huge rise in organized crime.

WOMEN ON THE BEAT
This is a uniform of a British woman police constable (WPC). The first female officers appeared on the streets in 1919, following the success of their voluntary patrols during World War I. They are now familiar sights patrolling the streets in company with a male officer, and must generally be in attendance when a female suspect is being arrested, questioned, or searched.

Hard hat, suitable for riot conditions

Handbag, fits WPC's truncheon

Traditional uniform used for ceremonial occasions – working uniform is brown

Tailored jackets and shirts replaced the previous issue which was more bulky

Headwear of a woman officer of the rank of Assistant Chief Constable

British woman's police hat

Indian police cap

British police helmet

British (1830s)   French (1920s)   Italian (1990s)

FROM OLD TO NEW
Although the job of the police to keep the peace has remained the same through time, both the uniforms and the technology available for use in the fight against crime have advanced a great deal. Compare the truncheon of the 1830s with the gun of the 1990s.

Police agencies

Sheriff's badge

Hungarian warrant card

IDENTIFICATION
All officers must carry identification. It is most important for plain-clothes officers. The identification displays the officer's details and photograph.

IT IS USUAL TO THINK of police as either the uniformed officers who keep the peace on the world's streets, or detectives who solve serious crimes. In fact, within police forces there are many specialized units formed to operate in special circumstances and conditions. Some squads are trained to deal with difficult violent situations, such as the Japanese riot police, the French Compagnies Republicaines de Securité (CRS) and the US Special Weapons and Tactics (SWAT) units. Others use specialized vehicles, such as helicopters, boats, motorcycles, or horses. The aim is to develop a chain of skills that can be used to defeat the criminal.

ON THE BEAT
A country's safety and well-being are usually in the hands of the "beat" officers such as the French policeman here. A beat police officer patrols the street on foot or in a car, preventing crime and protecting citizens' rights to a crime-free society.

Face protection against missiles

RECOVERING EVIDENCE
Many criminals seem to believe that throwing evidence – such as weapons – into a canal or river makes them disappear. However, most police forces have trained diving units. The officers of these units are called frogmen. Ninety-five per cent of a frogman's work is done in zero visibility, relying entirely on touch. In addition to weapons, cars, motorcycles, bodies are also found.

Underwater breathing apparatus

Armour to protect hands in close combat

Possible murder weapon

CROWD CONTROL
In any situation where rioting crowds cannot be managed by regular police, specially trained and equipped officers are sent to the scene to restore order. In Japan, the riot police (above) are known for their efficiency.

HIGHWAY PATROL
High speed and manoeuvrability have made motorcycles an essential vehicle for the police. Most forces have trained motorcycle units. The Los Angeles traffic police (left), for example, patrol the highways, motorways, and inner city areas.

POLICE MARKSMEN
Officers highly trained in the use of
firearms work with the regular police
in cases such as sieges or hostage
taking. The order to shoot to kill
is only given when all other
options have failed, as there
is always a chance of hitting
a civilian. These armed units
are separate from the many
officers throughout the world
who routinely carry guns.

*Unisex safety
helmet*

MOUNTAIN RESCUE
Special police teams with experience
of climbing are used in some
mountain areas to help in rescue
work. The officers (above) work
in the French Alps, and find
motorcycles ideal for travelling
quickly over rough ground. The
motorcycles are much lighter than
those used in highway patrol, and
are more like the "scramble" bikes
used in cross-country racing.

*High-velocity
rifle with
telescopic
sight*

*Officer's cape, for
use when it rains,
is kept in this
leather pouch*

*Police horses are played
loud recordings of crowds
and bands to get
them used to noise*

*Riders spend half their
working week grooming
horses and cleaning tack*

MOUNTED POLICE
Many countries have a
mounted police branch,
which is usually
confined to ceremonial
duties and crowd control.
The first British horse patrol
was a pair of mounted Bow
Street Runners (p. 10) in 1763. In 1805,
a larger patrol was introduced. Because
of the colour of their tunics, the officers
were called "Robin Redbreasts". Today
the Metropolitan Police has a patrol of
about 200 horses. One of their female
riders is shown here (right).

*Long baton
used in riot
control*

CANADIAN MOUNTIES
The Royal Canadian Mounted Police (Mounties)
were founded in 1873 to patrol the vast prairies
in the west. Today, they are one of the world's
most sophisticated and efficient police forces.
The intelligence and sure-footedness of the
horse makes it a perfect means of transport.

*Selected horses are
three- to four-year-old
hunters. Like their riders,
they receive about two
years' training*

Other detectives

THE TASK OF INVESTIGATING a crime, and identifying the culprit, is carried out by detectives. Whether by interviewing witnesses, or by searching for the tiniest piece of forensic evidence, detectives try to reconstruct a sequence of events until they believe they know what happened. Most detectives are officers in a specialized division of the police, but many others work for private agencies. These detectives, who are often known as private investigators (PIs), can be hired by anybody to investigate anything – for a daily fee. The public's fascination with the detection of crime is reflected in the number of detective stories in books, on film, and television. Whether these detectives are real-life or fictional characters, and no matter how much their methods and equipment differ, they share a common pursuit – the fight against crime.

SIR ARTHUR CONAN DOYLE
Probably the world's best-known detective is Sherlock Holmes, created in the 1880s by Conan Doyle (1859–1930), a British writer. Holmes relied on logical deduction and attention to minute detail to solve crimes. It is less well known that Conan Doyle was also an amateur sleuth himself, and was involved in a number of major cases.

TAKING A CLOSE LOOK
Sometimes the smallest details provide the clue that solves a crime, which is why being able to magnify objects is vitally important in detection. In the laboratory, microscopes are among the most valuable pieces of equipment. Detectives on surveillance must be able to see activities and people clearly, without being noticed themselves. In this instance, they will use a pair of binoculars.

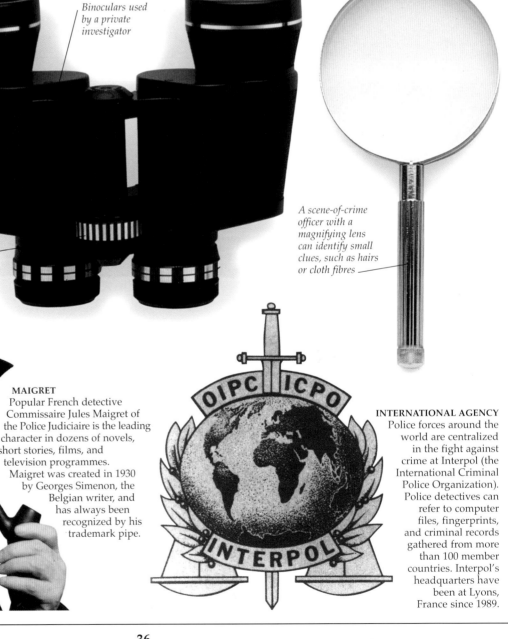

Binoculars used by a private investigator

This knob adapts the degree of magnification to suit different people's vision

A scene-of-crime officer with a magnifying lens can identify small clues, such as hairs or cloth fibres

MAIGRET
Popular French detective Commissaire Jules Maigret of the Police Judiciaire is the leading character in dozens of novels, short stories, films, and television programmes. Maigret was created in 1930 by Georges Simenon, the Belgian writer, and has always been recognized by his trademark pipe.

INTERNATIONAL AGENCY
Police forces around the world are centralized in the fight against crime at Interpol (the International Criminal Police Organization). Police detectives can refer to computer files, fingerprints, and criminal records gathered from more than 100 member countries. Interpol's headquarters have been at Lyons, France since 1989.

RAYMOND CHANDLER'S MARLOWE

A popular character in detective fiction is that of the hard-boiled, tough-talking private eye, who lives a lonely life on the city's "mean streets". Philip Marlowe, who was created by the author Raymond Chandler in the 1930s, is perhaps the best-known example of this type, immortalized in novels, films, and television.

MRS KERNER

Annette Kerner, Britain's most famous female private detective, worked from the early 1920s to 1950s. She became known as "the queen of disguise" and was equally convincing as a waitress in a criminals' café as she was as a society lady investigating a jewel theft. She once posed as a drug addict to catch a gang of opium dealers.

Allan Pinkerton

PRIVATE EYES THAT NEVER SLEEP

In 1850, US detective Allan Pinkerton established the organization which was to become the world's oldest privately owned detective agency – it is still going strong. The term "private eye" came from the Pinkerton trademark, the words "We Never Sleep" written under an open eye.

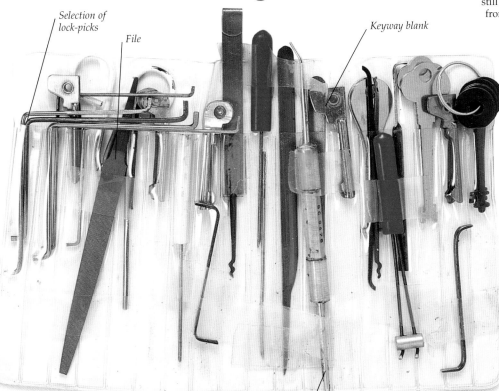

Selection of lock-picks

File

Keyway blank

Tool for probing locks

USING CRIME AGAINST CRIMINALS

It is not only burglars who find it useful to have a set of tools which opens locks. Many detectives and undercover surveillance officers also need to get past locked doors – perhaps in the search for drugs, stolen goods, or information about a crime. The official equipment shown on the left is capable of opening most kinds of lock, almost anywhere in the world.

Special telephoto lens for long-distance work

RECORDING EVIDENCE

All criminal investigations involve collecting a wide range of clues. In many cases, information collected on camera film is vital. It may provide evidence of a meeting between criminals, or a scene-of-crime record made before evidence is removed to a forensic laboratory. In most police forces, there are expert photographic teams.

PSYCHIC DETECTION

Estelle Roberts was a famous English "psychic" detective who worked with the police. Roberts believed she had a psychic gift. If she was given a personal object belonging to a crime victim, she could apparently imagine the crime scene and sometimes even the criminal's face.

Camera's standard lens

Undercover surveillance

IF YOU WANT TO PLAN A CRIME, or catch a criminal, information is vital. For example, the time at which a bank transfers money is as important for the bank robber, as the time of a planned raid is important to the law enforcement officer. In the early days of detective work, information-gathering techniques were simple. The robber, sometimes working with an accomplice inside the bank, would watch and wait. The officer, with the help of underworld informants, would do the same. Today, however, huge technological advances mean that gathering secret information has never been easier. With round-the-clock observation on closed circuit television, telephone tapping using tiny transmitters, and ultraviolet gel that leads detectives to the thief, criminals may be seen, heard, and traced through every stage of their crimes.

THE EVER-OPEN EYE
The invention of closed circuit television (CCTV) has been vital in the fight against crime. Signals are transmitted from a camera to a television screen along cables or telephone links, in a closed circuit. CCTV is used in places such as shopping precincts or banks. It can provide police with accurate records of people committing crimes and sometimes lead to visual identification. CCTV is used in law courts. The young and vulnerable can be interviewed in a separate room with a live video replay in the courtroom.

WIRED FOR SOUND
Below left is a battery-operated bug the size of a matchbox. It has a microphone attached to a radio transmitter, and is hidden in the place to be bugged. Sound signals from the bug are picked up by the radio receiver, which transfers the signals to an earpiece.

A BUGGED ELECTRIC SOCKET
This electric plug socket looks like any other. Even with the cover removed, the miniature bugging device is not visible. The device is a transmitter that carries sound in the room, in the form of radio waves, to a distant receiving unit. Another kind of device transmits sound directly along the power cable to a receiver plugged into the same electrical circuit.

Radio receiver with earpiece

CONCEALED CAMERA
This canvas shoulder bag has been adapted to hide a video camera. The catch to one of the fastenings has been removed, leaving a hole. The camera is carefully positioned inside the bag so that the lens sits next to the adapted fastening. This makes it possible to record images from within the bag without anyone realizing they are being filmed.

Ordinary canvas sports bag

Bag filled with clothing to protect the camera and hold it in position

Main body of bag has a hole in it, through which the camera lens receives an image

Normal-sized lens. Some cameras have lenses as small as match heads

Purse with transmitter

This wire clips to a document connecting it to an alarm which is activated if the document is disturbed

Alarm

Magnet to cancel alarm

DESK TRAP
These devices alert people to thieves attempting to steal from desk drawers. The lower device has two magnets joined by a wire. One magnet is stuck to the underside of the desk, the other to the top of the drawer. If the drawer is opened, the magnetic field is broken, setting off an alarm (top right).

Radio receiver

HIGH-TECH PURSE
If this wallet is moved, a radio transmitter triggers an alarm system. A thief trying to lift the purse from a bag or drawer would be detected immediately. A magnet passed across the wallet cancels the alarm.

Magnetic strip

STAKEOUT
A stakeout is an undercover surveillance operation. In this still from the film *Stakeout*, a detective keeps watch through binoculars. Detectives also use wiretaps and other classic devices to keep crucial witnesses and suspects under surveillance.

UV paste, which sticks well to metal

Cotton wool for applying powders

Paintbrush for applying pastes

UV crayons for marking furniture or boxes

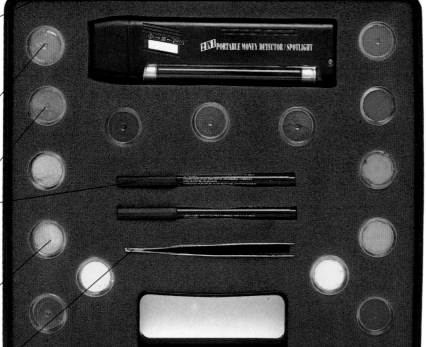

ULTRAVIOLET DETECTOR KIT
One way to fool burglars is to mark valuable goods with a substance that is invisible under normal lighting, but shows up clearly under ultraviolet light. The thief's hands become covered with the substance when handling the goods. Another trick is to use a substance that is colourless until it mixes with water. The thief touches the goods and unwittingly covers his or her hands with the substance. Gradually the moisture from the hands causes a reaction in the substance which becomes visible as a brightly coloured stain. Ultraviolet markers are also used to write the owner's name on their possessions. If the goods are stolen and recovered by the police, the owner can then be contacted.

Gloves protect detective's hands when applying

UV powder for wood or paper objects

Blue UV powder is used on blue objects

UV pen

Powders are visible when concentrated, but invisible once applied

Tweezers for holding banknotes or coins during application

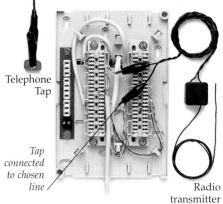

Telephone Tap

Tap connected to chosen line

Radio transmitter

TAPPING INTO CONVERSATIONS
Access to other people's conversations on the telephone is often useful. One method of tapping is to connect wires and a transmitter to the junction box outside the building. Another method is to fit a radio transmitter directly into the telephone handset, sending conversations to a receiver set.

Crime scene

EVERY CRIMINAL INCIDENT, no matter how minor, happens somewhere; this place is called the scene of the crime. The first job of police officers at the crime scene is to seal off the area so that potential evidence is not disturbed. Once this has happened, no unauthorized person is allowed into the area. The most important members of the investigation team at this point are the scene-of-crime officers (SOCOs) whose highly trained and experienced eyes will search for clues to be sent to the forensic science laboratory for examination. Forensic science is the technique of using scientific methods to solve crimes. Modern forensic science has its origin in 1910, when Edmond Locard of France formulated his "exchange theory". This states that criminals will always take something away from the scene of their crime, or leave something behind. The criminal may take away hair or blood from the victim or soil on the soles of his or her shoes. He or she may leave fingerprints, footprints, or fibres from clothing. It is this evidence that the SOCOs collect.

MURDER!
In the case of murder, the body of the victim must be removed from the crime scene and taken for postmortem as soon as possible. Before this can happen, the victim must be pronounced dead by a doctor. Then a forensic pathologist makes a preliminary examination. Next, a chalk or tape outline is made around the corpse so that investigators know its position. The body can then be transported to the hospital mortuary, where the postmortem takes place.

Toothed callipers enable a tight grip on wet or slippery articles

HUNTING FOR CLUES
This picture shows the hunt for information at the scene of a murder in New York, the United States. Nothing has been touched or moved to allow scene-of-crime experts and photographers to record as many details of the crime as possible. A police photographer is recording relevant evidence on film, while his colleague searches for evidence that may be sent to the forensic laboratory.

THE AMPEL PROBE
This tool was designed for use by crime scene investigators. The tongs enable officers to search suspects or their property without risking personal injury, for example, from an open knife, and without damaging objects that may bear trace evidence such as fingerprints. It is also useful for removing evidence without personal contact.

Specially designed handles ensure firm grip

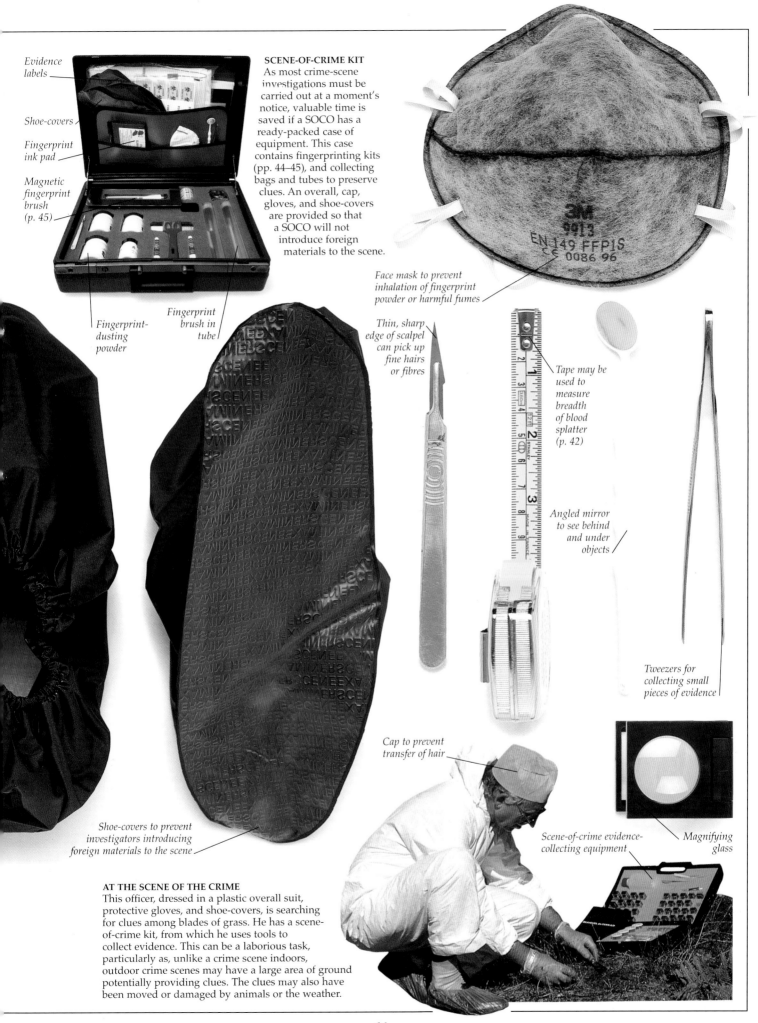

Evidence labels

Shoe-covers

Fingerprint ink pad

Magnetic fingerprint brush (p. 45)

SCENE-OF-CRIME KIT
As most crime-scene investigations must be carried out at a moment's notice, valuable time is saved if a SOCO has a ready-packed case of equipment. This case contains fingerprinting kits (pp. 44–45), and collecting bags and tubes to preserve clues. An overall, cap, gloves, and shoe-covers are provided so that a SOCO will not introduce foreign materials to the scene.

Fingerprint-dusting powder

Fingerprint brush in tube

3M
9913
EN 149 FFP1S
CE 0086 96

Face mask to prevent inhalation of fingerprint powder or harmful fumes

Thin, sharp edge of scalpel can pick up fine hairs or fibres

Tape may be used to measure breadth of blood splatter (p. 42)

Angled mirror to see behind and under objects

Tweezers for collecting small pieces of evidence

Shoe-covers to prevent investigators introducing foreign materials to the scene

Cap to prevent transfer of hair

Scene-of-crime evidence-collecting equipment

Magnifying glass

AT THE SCENE OF THE CRIME
This officer, dressed in a plastic overall suit, protective gloves, and shoe-covers, is searching for clues among blades of grass. He has a scene-of-crime kit, from which he uses tools to collect evidence. This can be a laborious task, particularly as, unlike a crime scene indoors, outdoor crime scenes may have a large area of ground potentially providing clues. The clues may also have been moved or damaged by animals or the weather.

Following clues

SEEMINGLY INSIGNIFICANT traces left at a scene of crime by the victim or criminal are vital clues that can help police in their investigations. These clues range from fingerprints, or tyre and shoe prints, which can help identify a criminal, to bloodstains that can illustrate where or how the crime took place. Investigating officers carefully analyze every aspect of a crime scene. Sometimes the clues would not be noticed by an untrained person. More dramatic evidence, such as bullet holes and broken glass, are easily noticed, but the analysis of these clues needs special training and equipment. The damage weapons cause can also provide clues. For example, a piece of glass shattered by a bullet may leave traces on a criminal's clothes.

DROPS OF BLOOD
To the specially trained SOCO (pp. 40–41), marks left by blood can be very revealing. From the shape of blood drops on a flat surface, it is possible to tell from what height they fell. Splashes on a wall can show the direction from which they came. Other patterns are spurts, pools, smears, and trails. These may reveal the movements of the victim and criminal, and help piece together details of the crime.

The fired bullet is propelled along the barrel, picking up marks on its way

BULLET MARKS
Cartridges consist of two parts, bullets and cases. When a gun is fired, the bullet travels along the barrel picking up marks unique to that gun, which can be compared with a test bullet fired from the same weapon. The same is true of marks left on the base of the cartridge case by the firing pin. A particular weapon can therefore be connected to a particular crime.

Marks left on the cartridge, caused by the firing pin when the gun is fired

SHOE PRINTS
Shoe prints are left either as impressions in a soft substance such as soil, or as prints in blood, paint, or oil. These traces are photographed at the scene for future comparison with the shoes of a suspect. Identification points may be the patterns on the sole, and distinctive signs of wear and tear.

TYRE PRINTS
Prints can be left by tyres in the same way as by shoes. They can be compared with the tyres on a suspect's car and, like shoes, often have an identifiable wear pattern. Police are further helped by the fact that manufacturers use different types of tyres on different models of car.

SHOTS THROUGH GLASS
The study of guns and ammunition is called ballistics. In a forensic laboratory specializing in ballistics, experts set up tests to demonstrate the effects caused by bullets fired from different distances and through different thicknesses of glass (above). This information is referred to when examining a bullet hole in glass from a crime scene. It helps build up a picture of where the gun was fired from.

Broken pattern in tyre print, suggesting two treads on the outer edge of the tyre have been worn down

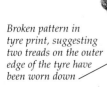

BREAKING GLASS
When glass is smashed, the broken edges have tiny shell-shaped notches. A broken window can be fitted together like a jigsaw puzzle. A piece of glass discovered in the suspect's car is compared to glass recovered from the crime scene. If the notches fit exactly, the glass is from the same window pane.

REFRACTIVE INDEX
Tiny pieces of glass found on a suspect's clothing may be too small to fit into a glass jigsaw. Instead, it can be compared to glass from the crime scene by measuring its refractive index, or the amount a ray of light bends when it passes through glass. Different kinds of glass have different refractive indexes.

DUST AND SOIL ANALYSIS
Because dust and soil are so easily carried from the crime scene – on shoes and clothing, in the hair and on the skin of a suspect – they are useful for comparison with similar substances at the scene. Dust and soil both vary greatly in their contents, often over a small area, so this analysis can prove quite accurate.

Crowbar used by a burglar to force open windows or doors

Wood chippings left at crime scene after chisel is used

Contents of hoover bag from suspect's home may contain dust samples that match those at crime scene

Dust

Soil

Plastic bag thrown away in suspect's home may contain a receipt revealing purchase of items found at the crime scene

CLUES IN RUBBISH
Wastepaper baskets and dustbins are routinely searched for evidence after a crime. For example, discarded documents, such as letters, may reveal a suspect's movements in the weeks leading up to the crime. Actual evidence, such as a weapon or stained clothing, may be found in a dustbin.

LOOKING AT DOCUMENTS
No two people's writing is the same. To a handwriting expert, just a scribbled note can be connected to a suspect whose writing is known. An apparently blank page may be indented from writing on the previous page, which has been torn off. This too can be used to identify a suspect.

Chisel, used to force open a lock

IN THE LABORATORY
Most forensic laboratories specialize in one particular branch of science, for example biology, chemistry, or ballistics. Some of the equipment is specific to that subject, but most laboratories rely heavily on comparison microscopes (pp. 46–47). The busy laboratory (left) is fairly typical. Most laboratories will have evidence from hundreds of crimes awaiting analysis.

IDENTIFYING TOOL MARKS
Tool marks are usually left at the scenes of burglaries, and have been made by an implement, or tool, used to force open a door or window. Because the tool is harder than the wooden frame, it will leave an impressed imprint of its shape. Sometimes this can be matched to an implement owned by a suspect – particularly if it has a distinctive shape, or has marks of previous damage.

Fingerprints and DNA

MANY EARLY civilizations were aware of the unique nature of the ridges and furrows on the tips of the fingers. Chinese potters, for example, signed their work with a fingerprint. However, it was not until 1858 that William Herschel, an English civil servant in India, claimed that no two person's fingerprints are the same, and that they do not change with age. During the late 19th century, researchers developed a method of classifying prints so that they could be easily identified. Just as fingerprints are unique to an individual's fingertips, so deoxyribonucleic acid (DNA) is unique to every cell of an individual's body. In 1984, scientists discovered how to create DNA profiles, sometimes called genetic fingerprints, from body fluids, flesh, skin, or hair roots. By matching the genetic information from a forensic sample with that of a suspect, investigators can prove a suspect guilty or innocent.

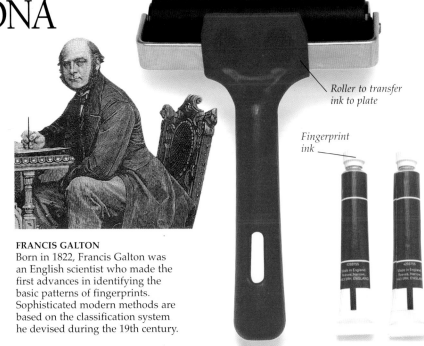

FRANCIS GALTON
Born in 1822, Francis Galton was an English scientist who made the first advances in identifying the basic patterns of fingerprints. Sophisticated modern methods are based on the classification system he devised during the 19th century.

Roller to transfer ink to plate

Fingerprint ink

INK AND ROLL
The universal method of taking a suspect's fingerprints is called ink and roll. A thin coating of black ink is rolled onto a metal plate. Then, one by one, each of the subject's fingertips is rolled on the ink from one side of the nail to the other, and on a white chart, producing prints.

Lifting tape to remove prints from surface

Aluminium dusting powder – photographs well as the powder reflects light

BRUSHING UP
If fingerprints have been left in a substance such as blood or paint, they are easy to see. However, most prints are made by the oils and sweat on the surface of the skin and are almost invisible. The most common technique for revealing these fingerprints is by dusting a fine powder over the surface, which sticks to the oily deposit. The powder-covered prints are removed from the surface on transparent sticky tape and then photographed. This officer is dusting for prints on a stolen car.

Fan-shaped brush for larger areas

Brush used with very fine powders

Long-handled brush for reaching into corners

Delicate "whisper" brush used with aluminium powder

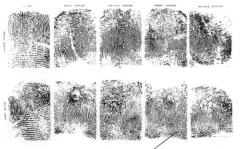

19th-century fingerprint chart

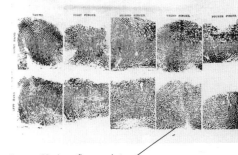

Various fingerprints

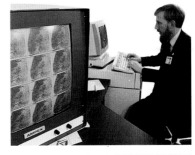

Arch

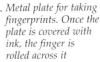

Loop

Whorl

Composite

CATALOGUING PRINTS

Fingerprint records are kept so that a suspect's prints, or fingerprints found at a crime scene, can be checked against any existing records. Checking is performed by specialists who look for points of similarity between the prints. In Britain, for example, 16 points of similarity must be found to confirm a match. This amount varies from country to country. As the number of fingerprint records has grown, a computer system has been developed which is able to store the records and compare more than 60,000 fingerprints per second.

FINGERPRINT PATTERNS

In the late 19th century, British police officer Edward Henry developed a system of classifying fingerprints. It stated that all fingerprints can be organized into four main types. "Arches" have ridges that run from one side of the finger to the other. With "loops", the ridges make a backward turn, and "whorls" have ridges that make a circle. Some prints include all three patterns and are called "composites".

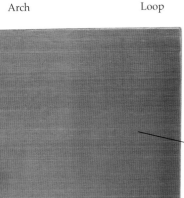

Metal plate for taking fingerprints. Once the plate is covered with ink, the finger is rolled across it

Special brush, composed of one magnetized tube within another. When the inner tube is pulled back, the magnet releases the particles

Alec Jeffreys looking at DNA samples

Palm print was made with a powder of aluminium filings

MAGNETIC PRINT

Many substances are used as dusting powders. The type used depends mainly on the surface on which the print has been left. For example, some powders are more suitable for sticky surfaces, while others are better for paper and cardboard.

EVIDENCE IN A MOLECULE

In 1984, Alec Jeffreys, an English scientist, made DNA the international standard for identification. He discovered that within a single DNA molecule there is a sequence of information unique to each individual (except identical twins, who have the same DNA). Like fingerprinting, DNA profiling can be used to connect a suspect with the scene of a crime.

BIOLOGICAL "PATTERN"

From a sample of any human tissue or body fluid, a biological "pattern" of that person can be created. This is called a DNA sample and looks like a supermarket bar code.

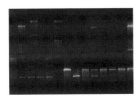

Forensic analysis

DESPITE DEVELOPMENTS in technology, the basic principles of forensic science have remained the same. A forensic scientist's main task is comparison. For example, the scientist will compare a hair found at a crime scene with one from a suspect's head, or match a fabric fibre found in a suspect's car with the clothing worn by a victim. The main techniques used are microscopic examination and chemical analysis. A forensic laboratory will use several types of microscopes in their work; electron microscopes can magnify objects more than 150,000 times, which makes identification and comparison more precise. Comparison microscopes are used, allowing a scientist to view two samples side by side. Other types of microscope can help compare bullets to determine their source, or identify minerals and drugs. Forensic laboratory work combines many different disciplines, such as biology, chemistry, ballistics (the study of guns and ammunition), and document analysis.

NAPOLEON'S DEATH
Napoleon Bonaparte's death in 1821 is ascribed to stomach cancer. However, there have been persistent rumours that he was poisoned. In 1960, a forensic team analyzed a lock of Napoleon's hair, taken from his head when he died. More than 13 times the normal level of arsenic was found. The poison could have been administered deliberately, or ingested by accident.

SEARCHING FOR SALIVA
Forensic scientists often look for evidence left at murder scenes. The pillow (above) has been sprayed with a substance that binds with protein. The protein will fluoresce under the laser torch, showing the presence of body fluids, such as saliva. The pillow can be then sent to the laboratory for DNA analysis (pp. 44–45).

Laser torch used to detect the presence of proteins, found in body fluids

Human eyebrow magnified 500 times

Green cotton fibres and yellow polyester fibres magnified 1,000 times

Dog hairs magnified 1,000 times

Extracting solvent absorbs poisons as urine sample is spun

IN THE LABORATORY
The forensic laboratory is one of the most valuable tools in a crime investigation. Clothing, shoe prints (pp. 40–41), dust traces, potential weapons, and bullets are a few examples of items collected for analysis. This scientist is using a comparison microscope. Originally designed for the comparison of bullets and cartridge cases, it is now used to compare almost any kind of evidence. Two slides carrying samples are placed on the viewing tray. The slides are viewed simultaneously through the eyepieces.

Centrifuge spins at a rate of 2,000 to 3,000 revolutions per minute

Scientist examines some fibres in an evidence bag under the microscope

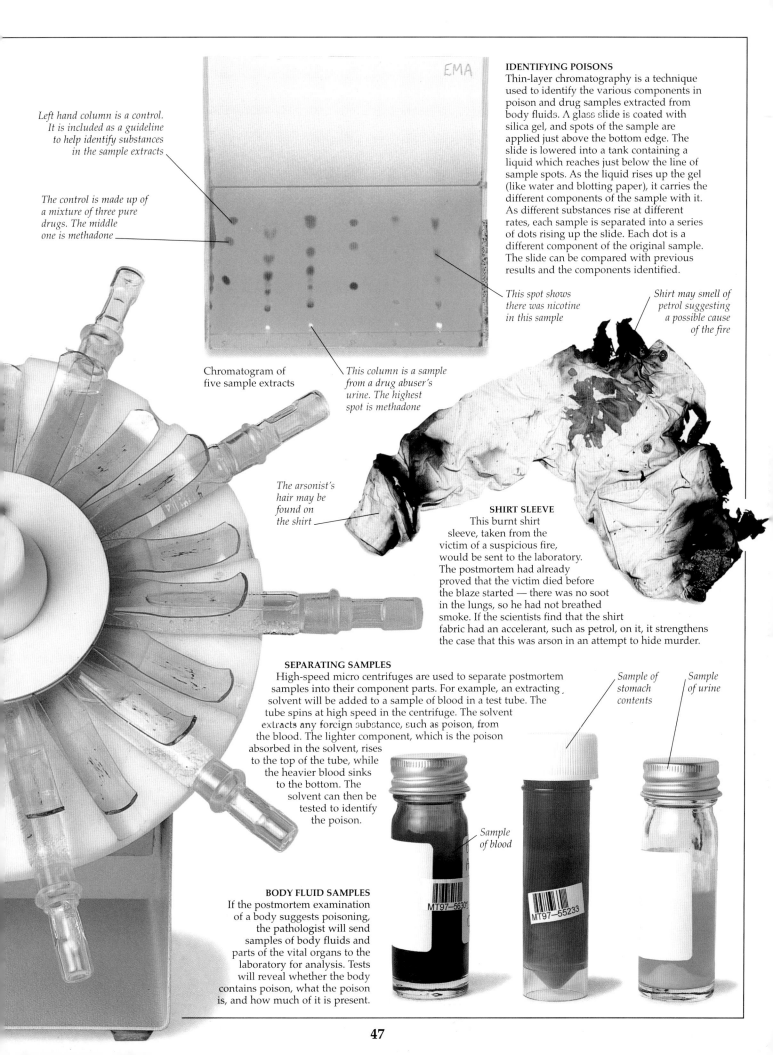

Left hand column is a control. It is included as a guideline to help identify substances in the sample extracts

The control is made up of a mixture of three pure drugs. The middle one is methadone

EMA

IDENTIFYING POISONS

Thin-layer chromatography is a technique used to identify the various components in poison and drug samples extracted from body fluids. A glass slide is coated with silica gel, and spots of the sample are applied just above the bottom edge. The slide is lowered into a tank containing a liquid which reaches just below the line of sample spots. As the liquid rises up the gel (like water and blotting paper), it carries the different components of the sample with it. As different substances rise at different rates, each sample is separated into a series of dots rising up the slide. Each dot is a different component of the original sample. The slide can be compared with previous results and the components identified.

Chromatogram of five sample extracts

This column is a sample from a drug abuser's urine. The highest spot is methadone

This spot shows there was nicotine in this sample

Shirt may smell of petrol suggesting a possible cause of the fire

The arsonist's hair may be found on the shirt

SHIRT SLEEVE

This burnt shirt sleeve, taken from the victim of a suspicious fire, would be sent to the laboratory. The postmortem had already proved that the victim died before the blaze started — there was no soot in the lungs, so he had not breathed smoke. If the scientists find that the shirt fabric had an accelerant, such as petrol, on it, it strengthens the case that this was arson in an attempt to hide murder.

SEPARATING SAMPLES

High-speed micro centrifuges are used to separate postmortem samples into their component parts. For example, an extracting solvent will be added to a sample of blood in a test tube. The tube spins at high speed in the centrifuge. The solvent extracts any foreign substance, such as poison, from the blood. The lighter component, which is the poison absorbed in the solvent, rises to the top of the tube, while the heavier blood sinks to the bottom. The solvent can then be tested to identify the poison.

Sample of stomach contents

Sample of urine

Sample of blood

BODY FLUID SAMPLES

If the postmortem examination of a body suggests poisoning, the pathologist will send samples of body fluids and parts of the vital organs to the laboratory for analysis. Tests will reveal whether the body contains poison, what the poison is, and how much of it is present.

MT97–56301

MT97–55233

47

The bare bones

FEW PEOPLE COULD EVEN GUESS how much information an expert can glean from a pile of bones – information that can help solve a crime. A skeleton can determine the gender of the deceased. Male and female skeletons have different skulls and pelvic (hip) bones. Even without a complete skeleton, height can be calculated within 25 mm (1 in) by measuring the long bones (the femur bone in the leg or the tibia bone in the arm). Age can sometimes be determined from the way in which sections of the skull have closed together, or, up to the age of 25, from the development of the teeth. The structure of the head, face, teeth, and long bones can also indicate to which indigenous group the deceased belonged.

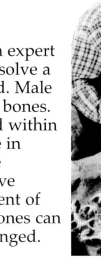

MIKHAIL GERASIMOV
The pioneers of facial reconstruction were Mikhail Gerasimov and Professor Grigoriev of Russia working during the 1950s. The reconstruction of Tamerlane the Great, the Mongol king, was Gerasimov's greatest achievement. In the illustration above, Gerasimov (left) and an archaeologist examine a 30,000-year-old skeleton.

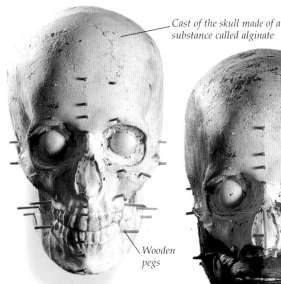

Cast of the skull made of a substance called alginate

Wooden pegs

Work starts with the temples and the neck

Building the nose is very demanding

1 The skeleton of a young woman was dug up in Wales in 1989 and named "Little Miss Nobody" by the police. Richard Neave began a facial reconstruction by making a cast of the skull. Then pegs are inserted at fixed points to indicate the standard thickness of the flesh.

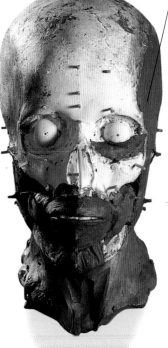

A male sacrum is narrower than a female sacrum

2 Plastic balls make "eyes" and the "flesh" is built up in clay. With the shape of the skull and the length of the pegs as guides, the muscles of the face begin to form.

3 After the mouth, the areas around the eye sockets are carefully filled in. Then the nose is formed. Because there are few bones that indicate the shape of the nose, this is one of the most difficult parts of the reconstruction.

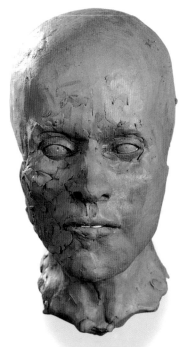

4 The clay has now been filled out to the tops of the guide pegs and the sculptor is ready to put the finishing touches to the head. All that remains is to smooth the surface to give a more lifelike appearance. If the age of the person at death is known, the sculptor can texture the skin correctly. The whole process takes little more than a day to complete.

HIS AND HERS
Men and women have different skeletons. Male skulls have a little lump at the back of the head called the nuchal crest and another on the forehead called the suborbital ridge. The sciatic notch on the hips is wider on the female skeleton than on the male. The sacrum, at the bottom of the spine, is smaller in males than females.

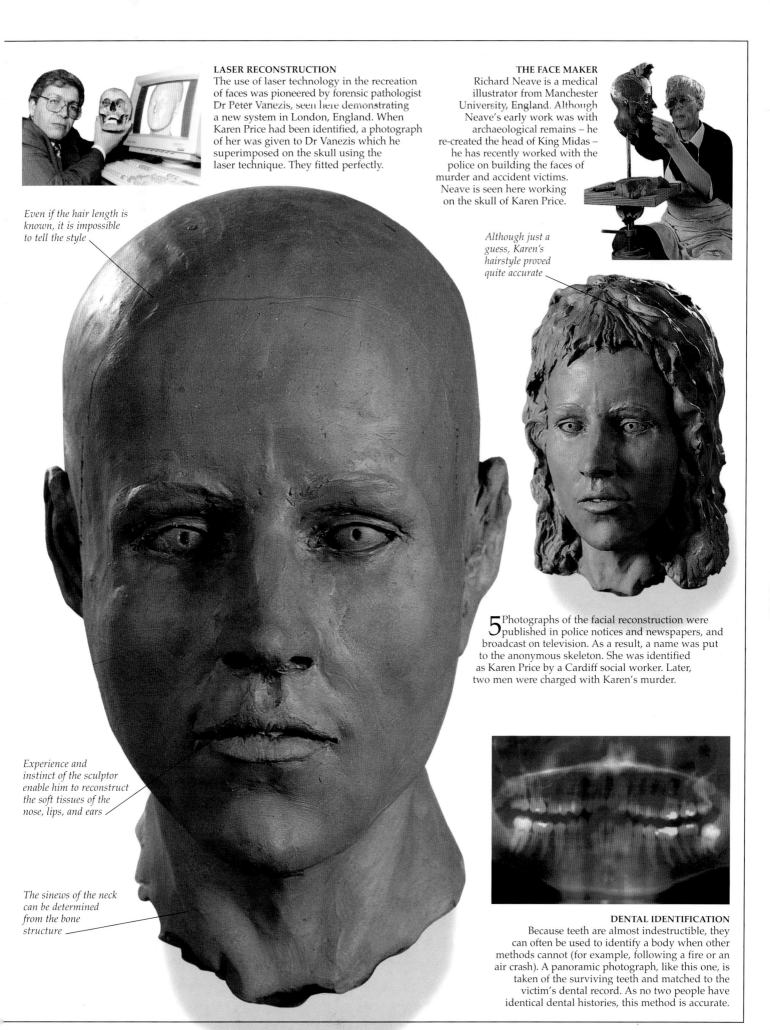

LASER RECONSTRUCTION
The use of laser technology in the recreation of faces was pioneered by forensic pathologist Dr Peter Vanezis, seen here demonstrating a new system in London, England. When Karen Price had been identified, a photograph of her was given to Dr Vanezis which he superimposed on the skull using the laser technique. They fitted perfectly.

THE FACE MAKER
Richard Neave is a medical illustrator from Manchester University, England. Although Neave's early work was with archaeological remains – he re-created the head of King Midas – he has recently worked with the police on building the faces of murder and accident victims. Neave is seen here working on the skull of Karen Price.

Even if the hair length is known, it is impossible to tell the style

Although just a guess, Karen's hairstyle proved quite accurate

5 Photographs of the facial reconstruction were published in police notices and newspapers, and broadcast on television. As a result, a name was put to the anonymous skeleton. She was identified as Karen Price by a Cardiff social worker. Later, two men were charged with Karen's murder.

Experience and instinct of the sculptor enable him to reconstruct the soft tissues of the nose, lips, and ears

The sinews of the neck can be determined from the bone structure

DENTAL IDENTIFICATION
Because teeth are almost indestructible, they can often be used to identify a body when other methods cannot (for example, following a fire or an air crash). A panoramic photograph, like this one, is taken of the surviving teeth and matched to the victim's dental record. As no two people have identical dental histories, this method is accurate.

Attention to detail

THERE ARE FEW "OPEN AND SHUT" cases – crimes where it is known immediately what happened, who did it, and why. Most successful cases rely on the investigators who put together a case from small clues. Often no detail is too insignificant. It may happen that a witness remembers the colour or make of a car, or better still its registration number. An onlooker may have noticed something about a suspect such as physical features, voice, or a distinctive tattoo, near the scene of the crime. Sometimes the criminal has a distinctive way of dressing or distinctive jewellery. These eyewitness details will be added to the other clues picked up by scene-of-crime officers and forensic scientists and built into a case to be presented later to a jury in court.

IDENTITY PARADE
Identity parades are police procedure throughout most of the world. A suspect takes any position in a line of innocent people of similar appearance. The witness is then asked to identify the suspect. Parades are not very reliable. If the real criminal is not there, a witness may choose someone who looks most like the criminal.

A "bar print" which represents the sound made by a person saying the word "baby".

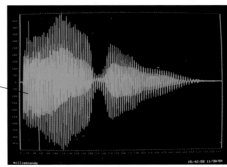

DISTINGUISHING MARKS
Members of gangs often like to have some way of identifying with fellow members. Tattoos are a good means of identification because they cannot easily be erased. Tattoos are always used by members of Chinese secret societies, such as Triads. Individually chosen tattoos are even more useful to the police, because no two people are likely to carry the same pattern of markings.

Death's head (skull) rings are popular with motorcycle gangs

VOICE RECOGNITION
The human voice has a unique "print". The system of recording and identifying voiceprints was developed during World War II. Above is a "bar print". The horizontal axis records the length of time, the vertical axis measures the strength of the sound. Voiceprints can be useful in identifying a suspect in cases of abusive telephone calls or demands over the telephone for ransom payments.

Photographic strips of eyes

Photographic strips of noses

A 19th century "mug-shot"

"MUG-SHOT" BOOK
Photography was invented in the mid-19th century. One of its most important uses was to allow police to keep visual as well as written records of criminals. This is one of the earliest examples of a "mug-shot" book, from the City of London Police. At that time, similar records were being kept in the United States, under the direction of Thomas Byrnes of the New York Police. In France, Alphonse Bertillon (pp. 52–53) was improving the French system by photographing both the front and side views of the criminal's head.

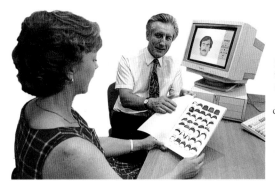

COMPUTER-AIDED VIDEOFIT

Improved computer technology has led to the videofit which replaces Photofit identification. Above, a witness is selecting the general hairstyle of the suspect. This is transferred to the video screen and can be altered to give a closer likeness. Another recent development can make the videofit three-dimensional so that it can be seen and changed at every angle.

REGISTRATION PLATES

All countries have a system of linking vehicles to their owners. This information can be used by the police to check whether a vehicle has been stolen, if it has been reported at a crime scene, and to find out details of the owner. Many criminals put false plates on cars to avoid detection. The British plate above is false. The numbers are too small and thick, making them difficult to read. The middle plate is a temporary French plate. The letters "WW" show it was issued to a person moving house.

False British plate

Temporary French plate

German export plate

These numbers indicate that the vehicle should have left the country by September 1996

Billions of different faces can be made up by combining the various strips

One strip that will make the nose of a Photofit

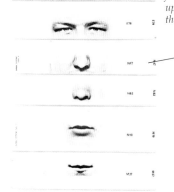

SELECTING EACH FEATURE

From this selection of just two pairs of eyes, two noses, and two mouths from a Penry Photofit kit, it can be seen how much features differ. The kits have about 100 different eyes, noses, and mouths. This still only represents a small proportion of the huge variety that exists of people's features. Unlike the videofit, Photofit just gives the "feeling" or "look" of a person, rather than a close representation.

A photographic strip of someone's hairline

The Photofit

The original subject

PHOTOFIT CASE

In 1971, Britain introduced the Penry Facial Identification Technique (Photofit). Jacques Penry's kit consisted of photographic strips of different eyes, noses, mouths, jaw lines, hairlines, and ears. These could be put together by the witness of a crime and a police expert. The resulting Photofit was put on display in public, often leading to a conviction.

MAKING UP A FACE

To show how the Photofit system works, a "witness" was shown an ordinary member of the public (above) and then asked to help in making the portrait, (above left) from memory. In a real crime situation, a traumatized witness may not remember the exact appearance of a criminal. So eyewitness identification has become devalued.

Criminal characteristics

For hundreds of years scientists have investigated the theory that certain people are born to be criminals. In the mid-19th century, anthropology, the study of humankind, became a popular science. Anthropologists studying the field of abnormal behaviour examined various types of criminal to see if they shared any physical characteristics. One of the foremost researchers was a French prison doctor called Lauvergne, who made plaster casts of his patients' heads to demonstrate their "evil" features. Most of Lauvergne's work was found to be incorrect. However, at the same time Alphonse Bertillon, working for the Paris police force, was also taking detailed measurements of criminals' heads and bodies, but for a different purpose. He was using the measurements to identify known criminals, rather than to create a physical profile of a criminal type.

WITCH HUNTS
In medieval times, it was thought that all witches had certain characteristics, such as warts or moles. Women thought to be witches were subjected to the "ducking" chair – being immersed in water while tied into a chair. If they did not drown, it was thought to prove they were witches, and they were executed anyway.

"SHERLOCK HOLMES OF THE COUCH"
Dr James Brussel was a US psychiatrist of the mid-20th century. Once described as the "Sherlock Holmes of the couch", he believed that by studying the way in which a crime was carried out, it was possible to describe the type of person who committed it. Dr Brussel used his theory successfully in helping to solve crimes. For example, he solved New York's "Mad Bomber" case (below) in 1957, and helped catch Albert de Salvo, the "Boston Strangler", in 1963.

According to Gall, the brain is divided into seven main sections which have different purposes, for example, intellectual or domestic

Within each main section, there are a number of areas that represent different functions, such as friendship and courage

PHRENOLOGY
In 1796, Dr Franz Gall, a doctor in Vienna, Austria, announced his theory of phrenology, the study of areas of the brain and their respective functions. According to Gall, while people were thinking, their brains changed shape, causing bumps on the surface of the skull. Phrenologists thought a person's character could be understood by studying the bumps. This mock-science was initially popular, but was soon rejected as false.

THE MAD BOMBER
In 1940, George Metesky began a 16-year series of bombing raids to seek revenge on his previous employer, who he believed had wronged him. It was the accurate psychological description of Metesky, given by Dr James Brussel, that led to Metesky's arrest. Although Metesky never killed anyone in his attacks, he was imprisoned.

CESARE LOMBROSO
An Italian psychiatrist of the mid-19th century, Cesare Lombroso made a study of 7,000 criminals in order to prove that there were different "criminal types" which could be identified by physical characteristics. For example, he believed that swindlers and bandits have larger heads than normal, and thieves and highwaymen had thick hair and beards. He never proved his theories despite the elaborate instruments he invented in order to do so.

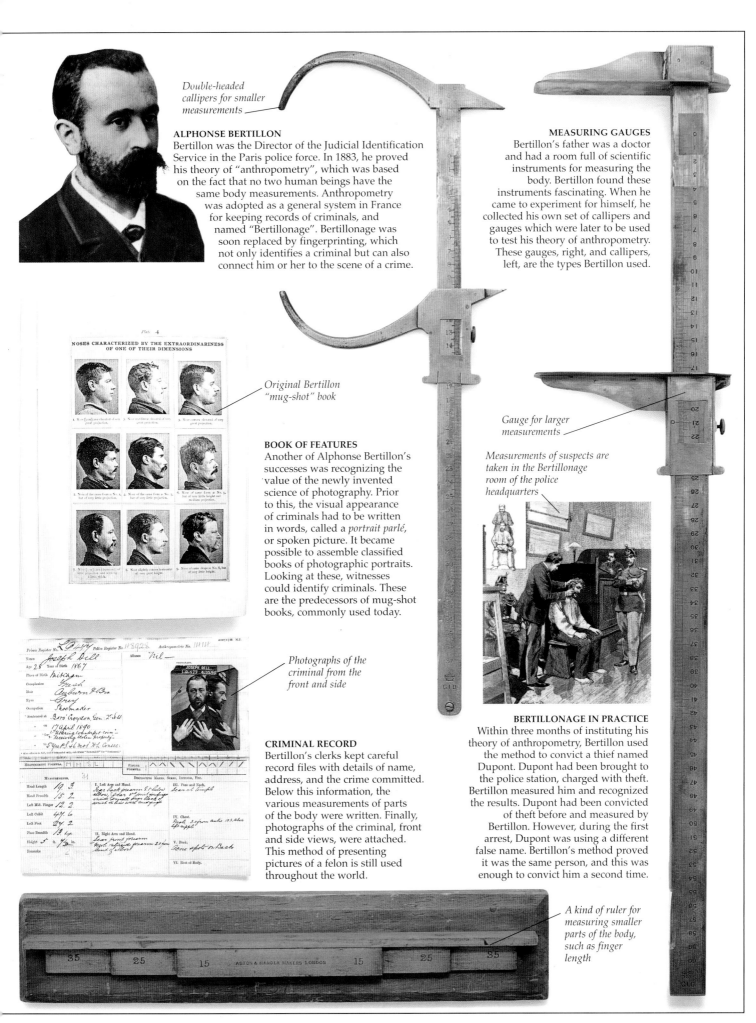

Double-headed callipers for smaller measurements

ALPHONSE BERTILLON

Bertillon was the Director of the Judicial Identification Service in the Paris police force. In 1883, he proved his theory of "anthropometry", which was based on the fact that no two human beings have the same body measurements. Anthropometry was adopted as a general system in France for keeping records of criminals, and named "Bertillonage". Bertillonage was soon replaced by fingerprinting, which not only identifies a criminal but can also connect him or her to the scene of a crime.

MEASURING GAUGES

Bertillon's father was a doctor and had a room full of scientific instruments for measuring the body. Bertillon found these instruments fascinating. When he came to experiment for himself, he collected his own set of callipers and gauges which were later to be used to test his theory of anthropometry. These gauges, right, and callipers, left, are the types Bertillon used.

Original Bertillon "mug-shot" book

NOSES CHARACTERIZED BY THE EXTRAORDINARINESS OF ONE OF THEIR DIMENSIONS

BOOK OF FEATURES

Another of Alphonse Bertillon's successes was recognizing the value of the newly invented science of photography. Prior to this, the visual appearance of criminals had to be written in words, called a *portrait parlé*, or spoken picture. It became possible to assemble classified books of photographic portraits. Looking at these, witnesses could identify criminals. These are the predecessors of mug-shot books, commonly used today.

Gauge for larger measurements

Measurements of suspects are taken in the Bertillonage room of the police headquarters

Photographs of the criminal from the front and side

CRIMINAL RECORD

Bertillon's clerks kept careful record files with details of name, address, and the crime committed. Below this information, the various measurements of parts of the body were written. Finally, photographs of the criminal, front and side views, were attached. This method of presenting pictures of a felon is still used throughout the world.

BERTILLONAGE IN PRACTICE

Within three months of instituting his theory of anthropometry, Bertillon used the method to convict a thief named Dupont. Dupont had been brought to the police station, charged with theft. Bertillon measured him and recognized the results. Dupont had been convicted of theft before and measured by Bertillon. However, during the first arrest, Dupont was using a different false name. Bertillon's method proved it was the same person, and this was enough to convict him a second time.

A kind of ruler for measuring smaller parts of the body, such as finger length

Following a scent

DOGS HAVE A SUPERIOR SENSE OF SMELL to humans and this has made them useful colleagues in the police fight against crime. By following a unique and invisible smell, dogs are able to track down a human's whereabouts. Police forces have developed ways of specially training dogs to chase after, grab, and hold a suspect, and then release them on command. Dogs have been used in tracking down criminals for a long time. Evidence of their use in 19th-century Britain can be found in the writings of Charles Dickens and Arthur Conan Doyle, and in the United States, dogs were often used to hunt escaped convicts and runaway slaves. During the 20th century, the role of the canine detective has been further expanded. Police, and other law enforcement agencies, now train dogs to sniff out drugs and explosives.

BLOODHOUNDS
Traditionally, tracking human beings was the bloodhound's special skill. However, they have now been superseded by lighter, more agile breeds. Commissioner Sir Charles Warren first brought bloodhounds in to London's Metropolitan Police in the 1880s. To test the bloodhounds' ability, Sir Charles acted as quarry to see if the dogs could track him down. They did – and one of them bit him!

CHECKING A CAR
A vast number of vehicles travel around the world on ships and ferries. At ports, sniffer dogs have been trained by port authorities to inspect vehicles for illegal substances such as drugs. Here, a dog is checking the engine compartment of a car.

SUSPICIOUS SUITCASE
Air transport presents similar smuggling problems. Dogs are used to search baggage holds. They are trained to recognize and detect scents of a range of contraband items, such as drugs or bomb-making equipment. If a suspicious suitcase is located by the dog, it alerts its handler.

SUPER SENSE
All around the world customs and excise authorities (pp. 28–29) use dogs to sniff out illicit chemicals. Common breeds used to hunt out substances such as cocaine and marijuana include springer and cocker spaniels and Labrador retrievers. However, sniffer dogs are not just used to hunt for drugs. The Department of Agriculture in the United States has its own "Beagle Brigade" to search for illicit fruit and meat in US airports.

Springer spaniel wears reflector harness when working in restricted light

Most popular police dog breed is the German Shepherd

SPECIAL TRAINING
Only puppies with good temperaments are selected for the rigorous training that must be gone through to become a police dog. A 14-week-old puppy is given to a handler who takes it home to become part of the family. When it is one year old, the dog is given 14 weeks of basic training where it is taught to obey voice and hand signals and how to track and hold a fugitive. The training also involves fitness exercises to build the dog's stamina and agility.

REX III
Perhaps the best-known of all police dogs was Rex III from England in the 1950s. His exploits, and those of his handler, are almost legendary. Rex III made more than 130 "arrests", was the first dog to work with the famous Flying Squad, and the first to be trained to detect drugs. During his active service, Rex III was awarded many honours and medals.

FINDING A VICTIM
During the blitz of London in World War II, sniffer dogs were used to locate people buried beneath the debris of bombed buildings. It is a job they still often perform in the ruins of earthquakes. Dogs are also used in murder inquiries to locate the victim's body.

Camera and lights

Harness is specially designed to be comfortable and lightweight

ON THE TRAIL OF A SUSPECT
Like police horses (pp. 34–35), dogs are trained to ignore loud noises such as gunfire. During their training, police dogs are taught the best way to attack, and how to avoid being clubbed by a weapon. Sadly, many brave animals are still killed in the line of duty.

Battery pack to power lights and camera

LIGHTS, CAMERA, ACTION
Trained sniffer dogs have another advantage over human detectives – they can search very small spaces. This dog is going to search a small area on the other side of a trap door. So that its handler can also see inside, the animal is fitted with a special harness with a small video camera, lights, and battery pack attached to it.

Instructor wears protective padding

ARRESTED BY A DOG
Police dogs are taught only to attack a suspect on the command of their handler. During their training, an instructor plays the part of a fleeing victim. Police dogs learn how to restrain a quarry by the arm, with the instructors wearing heavily padded sleeves to prevent injury. Despite their efficiency when attacking, police dogs have gentle natures.

Dog will practise attacking many times during training

Anti-heroes

It is a strange fact that some of the worst criminals in history have been turned into popular folk-heroes. One of the best examples is Dick Turpin (p. 14), a murderous thug who terrorized travellers in the countryside around London during the 18th century. He became a romantic figure after the publication of *Rookwood* (1834), a novel in which Turpin is portrayed as a chivalrous highwayman riding his trusty horse Black Bess. It is this idealized image that has stayed in the public's mind. Books are not the only reason for this hero-worship. There is a longing for the freedom of an outlaw, and an admiration for his or her daring. More recent anti-heroes range from the Great Train Robbers (p. 17) to India's Bandit Queen (below).

ROBIN HOOD
England's most famous hero Robin Hood is a legendary outlaw who robbed the rich and gave to the poor. There is no evidence that he actually existed; the stories of Robin's adventures are based on medieval ballads that have been embellished through the centuries. He has remained popular and even become the subject of numerous films, such as *The Adventures of Robin Hood* (above).

LOUIS MANDRIN
Louis Mandrin was one of the best-loved smugglers that France has ever known. In the 1740s, he formed a gang of 2,000 men, who were so well trained that they often defeated the king's troops. Mandrin's dashing adventures made him the people's hero. He was captured in 1755 and was executed by being tied to a large wheel, having his limbs crushed as the wheel turned, and then being left to die.

BUTCH AND SUNDANCE
Butch Cassidy and the Sundance Kid were members of the outlaw gang the Wild Bunch, who operated in the 1890s in the western United States. From their hideout Hole in the Wall, they specialized in large-scale horse and cattle rustling, and armed robberies of banks and trains. These outlaw gangs were always popular with the public, but Butch and Sundance became particularly well known after a highly romanticized film was made in the 1970s (right).

Butch was the leader of the Wild Bunch

Sundance's real name was Harry Longbaugh

Butch Cassidy's real name was Robert LeRoy Parker

THE BANDIT QUEEN
Phoolan Devi, also known as the Bandit Queen, was imprisoned in 1983 in India for banditry and murder. A rebel against her fate as a low-caste woman, Devi became a heroine to thousands of Indians. Once released, she fought politically for women's rights.

Front section of
Bonnie Parker's
body armour

*Bonnie's body
armour was found
on the ground near
the car in which she
and Clyde were shot*

Back section of
Bonnie Parker's
body armour

*Bonnie and Clyde
had removed their
body armour while
they ate their lunch*

*A bullet hole made
during the final
shoot out*

*Body armour
made of bullet-
proof material*

Floyd Hamilton's rifle

CLYDE BARROW
Clyde Barrow was born into
a poor Texas family in 1909.
He was already under arrest
for robbery when he met
19-year-old Bonnie Parker
in 1930. Two years later,
the pair began their
dramatic but short-
lived partnership.

*Miniature boots made
by Clyde Barrow for
his mother*

Clyde Barrow's watch

BONNIE AND CLYDE
In 1932, Clyde Barrow teamed up with
Bonnie Parker to become the most infamous
pair of robbers and murderers of the decade.
They terrorized the southwestern states of
the United States, murdering at least 13
people. In 1934, Bonnie and Clyde were
ambushed by police officers, who killed
them by firing 150 gun shots into their car.

*Photographs of
Blanche Barrow*

GANG MEMBERS
Clyde's brother Buck and
sister-in-law Blanche were also
members of the gang along
with robber Floyd Hamilton.
Buck was shot dead in 1933,
while Blanche was captured
and imprisoned. In 1938,
Hamilton was sentenced to
20 years in Alcatraz (pp. 12–13).

*A "Wanted"
poster put out
for Bonnie
and Clyde*

*Blanche wrote
of her advancing
blindess in later
years on the back
of this photograph*

Strange but true

CRIME AND THE LAW are serious subjects. However, crime also has its share of lighter moments and strange stories. Sometimes criminals are just foolish – such as armed robber Jose Sanchez. In 1995, police arrived at the scene of an armed robbery in New Jersey, the United States and found a piece of paper which the robber had used to wedge open the door of the building. It turned out to be a traffic ticket issued to Sanchez the night before the offence, which had his name and home address printed on it. There are other crimes that are strange because of the daring or ingenuity of the criminals, or because of the motives that inspired them. For example, John Hinckley attempted to assassinate President Reagan of the United States in 1981 in an attempt to impress actress Jodie Foster, with whom he was obsessed.

LINDOW WOMAN
In 1983, a badly decomposed female head was dug up at Lindow Moss in Cheshire, England. Frightened by the discovery, a local man confessed to the police that he had killed his wife 23 years before and buried her in the peat bog. In fact, when the remains were scientifically dated, they were found to be over 1,770 years old.

ON BOTH SIDES OF THE LAW
Welshman Henry Morgan was a famous 17th century buccaneer in the Caribbean. With the unofficial support of the English government, he spent over ten years attacking Dutch and Spanish colonies in the area. In 1670, Morgan raided Spanish-owned Panamá. Because the raid took place after a peace treaty between England and Spain, he was arrested, transported to London, and charged with piracy. Relations with Spain soured, and King Charles II knighted and pardoned Morgan, sending him back to Jamaica as deputy governor.

AVENGING "NAILS" MORTON'S DEATH
Dion O'Banion (above) was one of Chicago's most notorious gangsters, and Samuel "Nails" Morton was his most loyal gunman. Morton had been awarded the Croix de Guerre during active service in World War I and was considered indestructible. However, while out riding in Lincoln Park, Morton was thrown by a horse and killed. In revenge, O'Banion sent gunmen to kill the horse.

Tilh was tried, found guilty, and hanged

Film Sommersby *is loosely based on the story of Martin Guerre*

FAKE IDENTITY
After having disappeared for eight years, Martin Guerre returned in 1556 to his home in the French village of Artigat. He was welcomed by all except his uncle, who insisted that this Martin was an impostor. Guerre's uncle was right. Arnaud du Tilh had met Martin, got a detailed picture of his life, and adopted his identity. Tilh almost got away with it, but the real Martin Guerre returned.

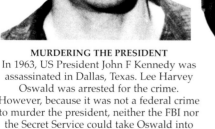

MURDERING THE PRESIDENT
In 1963, US President John F Kennedy was assassinated in Dallas, Texas. Lee Harvey Oswald was arrested for the crime. However, because it was not a federal crime to murder the president, neither the FBI nor the Secret Service could take Oswald into custody. Instead he was taken to a Dallas county jail, where, because of bad security, he was shot dead before he was put on trial.

*JSG Boggs'
drawing of an
English five-
pound note*

FORGER OR ARTIST

In October 1986, JSG Boggs, a US artist, was showing
his work at London's Young Unknowns Gallery.
To everyone's surprise, the police arrived and
seized the work. The reason was that the
drawings were of English banknotes. The Bank
of England prosecuted under the Forgery and
Counterfeiting Act, but Boggs was acquitted.

ESCAPE FROM THE COURT ROOM

On the night of 17 July 1976, Albert Spaggiari burgled the
bank Société Générale in Nice, France, after breaking in
through the underground sewer system. Captured and
put on trial for his crime, Spaggiari made a dramatic leap
from the dock and slipped out of a window. During his
12 years on the run, Albert Spaggiari hid behind
ridiculous homemade disguises like the one above.

JSG Boggs holding some of
his drawings of banknotes

*Italian, US, and
English banknotes*

BUTTERFLY LAW

Most countries have rules about killing
certain wildlife. In California, there is
a law specifically about butterflies.
City Ordinance Number 352 in Pacific
Grove states that it is a misdemeanour
to "kill or threaten a butterfly",
such as the swallowtail above.

INTERNET SWEET SHOP

While playing on the internet on his parents' computer,
a 15-year-old boy from Dublin, Ireland, came across a US
company offering mail order chocolate deliveries. The
company asked for a credit card number and, as a joke, the
boy made one up. Unfortunately, it was the real number of
someone in Argentina and $2,000 worth of chocolate arrived
at the boy's home. The culprit, as a juvenile, was not charged.

"TITANIC" THOMPSON

In April 1912, the liner
Titanic struck an iceberg off
Newfoundland with a loss of
1,513 lives. One who did not
perish was Alvon Clarence
Thompson. Women and
children had priority in the
escape, so Thompson dressed in
women's clothing to make sure
of a place in a lifeboat. Back in
the United States, Thompson
began to collect on the insurance
policies of the *Titanic*'s victims,
claiming them as relatives.

Index

Acknowledgements

Dorling Kindersley would like to thank: David Roberts; Ross Simms and the Winchcombe Folk and Police Museum; Sam Tree of Keygrove Marketing Ltd; Assistant Divisional Officer Derek Thorpe and the Fire Investigation Unit at Acton Police Station; Rentokil Pest Control; Dr Brian Widdop of the Medical Toxicology Unit Laboratory; Shona Lowe of HM Customs and Excise; The Metropolitan Police Museum; Mike Wombwell; the Commissioner for the City of London Police for his kind permission to photograph Penry's Photofit Kit; Bill Harriman of JWF Harriman **Researcher:** Robert Graham **Design and editorial coordinators:** Vicky Wharton, Jayne Parsons, Miranda Smith

Design and editorial assistance: Goldberry Broad, Darren Troughton, Jake Williamson, Julie Ferris, Nancy Jones, Susila Baybars

Additional photography: Geoff Dann, Gary Ombler; Richard Shellabear **Photographic assistance:** Gary Ombler, Andy Kamorovski, Tim John **Index:** Marion Dent **Jacket:** Mark Haygarth

Picture Credits:

The publisher would like to thank the following for their kind permission to reproduce their photographs:
a=above; b=below; c=centre; l=left; r=right; t=top:
Action Plus: Glyn Kirk 18cl; **Archive Photos:** 19ca, 24tr; Lambert 19r; **Archive Photos France:** 21ca, 35tr; **J.S.G. Boggs:** 59tl; **The British Council:** Anita Corbin & John O'Grady 45clb; **The British Film Institute:** © Warner Bros. 56tr; **The British Museum:** 14tr, 20tr, 20cb, 20crb, 21cr; **Bruce Coleman Collection:** Luiz Claudio Marigo 28br; **Camera Press:** Lionel Cherrualt 50cl; Dennis Stone 29tl; **Christies Images:** 22bc; **Corbis:** Bettmann 14bl, 14br, 37tr; Bettmann/UPI 24bl, 24br, 25tl, 25br, 52tr, 52cr; Everett 36bl; **Courtesy of Diners Club International:** 19c; **ET Archive:** British Museum 12tr; Tate Gallery 20br; **Mary Evans Picture Library:** 8tl, 10br, 11cl, 12tl, 13tl, 14cr, 14bc, 16bl, 19cb, 22tr, 22cl, 24cl, 28cl, 28bl, 29br, 36tl, 44tc, 45tl, 46tl, 52bl, 52br, 53crb; Explorer 9tl; **Fortean Picture Library:** Dr Elmar R. Gruber 9tr; **The Ronald Grant Archive:** © United Artists 37tl; © Warner Bros. 58bc; **Robert Harding Picture Library:** 34bl; FPG International 31tl; **David Hoffman:** 29tc, 31cr, 45tr; **Hulton Getty:** 8cl, 8cra, 8bl, 11tl, 16tl, 16cr, 17tl, 17tr, 18tr, 23tl, 23tc, 23tr, 23cl, 23cra, 33br, 53tl, 56cl; **The Image Bank:** Barros & Barros 40tr; **The Kobal Collection:** © Touchstone Pictures 39cra; © 20th Century Fox 50tr, 56br; **H. Keith Melton:** 37c; **Metropolitan Police Service:** 34br, 35c, 54cl, 55tl; **Microscopix:** Andrew Syred 46cll, 46cl, 46c; **Moviestore Collection:** © United Artists 15cl; **News International Associated Services:** 21br, 23crb; **Rex Features:** 42crb, 54bl, 59c; Hugh Routledge & Peter Bennett 51tl; Nils Jorgensen 43bc; Julian Makey 55cra, 55br; James Morgan 55c; John Shelley 35bl; Sipa/Dieter Ludwig 56bl; The Times 35tl; Today 46bc, 47cr; **Science Photo Library:** 49br; American Science and Engineering 29tr; Klaus Guldbrandsen 45bl; Peter Menzel 40clb, 46tr; Hank Morgan 50cr; **Service de l'Information et des Relations Publiques:** Tanguy Delamotte 34tr; **Frank Spooner Pictures:** 59tr; Gamma/G. Bassignac 41br; Georges Merillon 54 cb; Olivier Pighetti 15tl, 15tr; Olympia/Palazzotto 27tl; Sygma: Rufo 27cr; Sion Touhig 55tr; **Telegraph Colour Library:** 30tl; Ron Chapple 44bl; Colorific/Tim Graham 33brr, 34cl; **Topham Picturepoint:** 12bl, 12cr, 37tc, 37bl, 48tr, 58bl, 58cl, 58cr; Associated Press 25bl, 26bl, 26br, 27tr, 26tr; Press Association 49tl; Roger-Viollet: 8br, 36br; **Jerry Young:** 48cll, 48cl, 48cr, 48br, 49tr, 49c, 49cr.

Jacket: Hulton Getty: inside front bc.

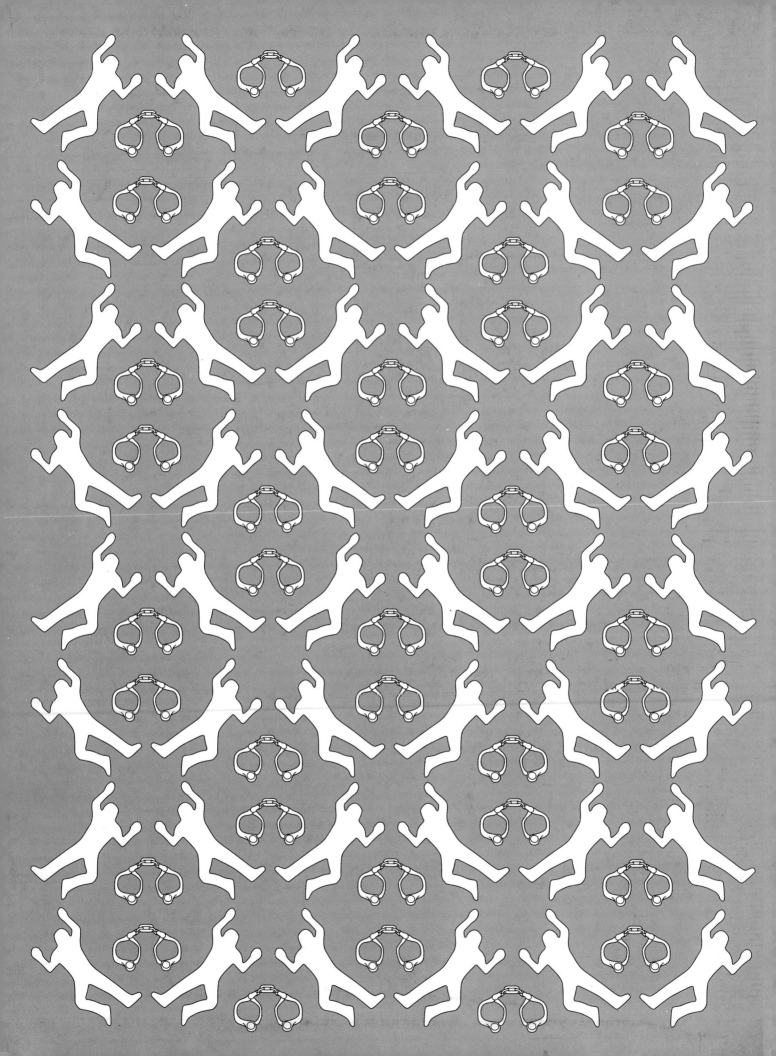